How Good Is Your Chess?

How Good Is Your Chess?

RATE YOUR SKILL AND IMPROVE YOUR STRATEGY
BY PARTICIPATING IN 35 MASTER GAMES

LEONARD BARDEN

Former British Chess Champion and
England International, Chess Correspondent,
The Guardian, The Field, Financial Times,
and *London Evening Standard*

Dover Publications, Inc., New York

Published in Canada by General Publishing
Company, Ltd., 30 Lesmill Road, Don Mills,
Toronto, Ontario.
Published in the United Kingdom by Constable
and Company, Ltd.

This Dover edition, first published in 1976, is an
unabridged republication of the work originally
published by Routledge and Kegan Paul, London,
in 1957.

International Standard Book Number: 0-486-23294-8
Library of Congress Catalog Card Number: 75-28848

Manufactured in the United States of America
Dover Publications, Inc.
180 Varick Street
New York, N.Y. 10014

TO

JONATHAN, PETER, AND RAAPHY

Author's Note

I would like to express my warmest thanks to my friend Daniel Castello for his kindness and care in reading the proofs.

vi

CONTENTS

Page

vii

CONTENTS

HOW TO RATE YOUR SCORE

Average score on eight games	U.S., British, or international rating	What this rating means
45–50	2400(225) up	Master or grandmaster strength; good enough to qualify for the U.S. championship or do well in the British championship; consider turning professional!
40–44	2300(212)–2399(224)	High score in U.S. Open, British championship, or major international opens.
35–39	2200(200)–2299(211)	British championship standard; winner local weekend opens; club or state champion.
30–34	2100(187)–2199(199)	Strong club player; 50 percent scorer in national opens; possible U.S. Amateur champion.
25–29	2000(175)–2099(186)	Upper board club player; 50 percent on a good week in national opens; if aged under 16, potential junior international player.
15–24	1800(150)–1999(174)	Above-average club player.
8–14	1400(100)–1799(149)	Home or occasional player up to moderate club player.
0–7	Below 1400(100)	Beginner or near-beginner; try to play in chess clubs and weekend opens for match experience.

INTRODUCTION

MANY chess players find that they lack the time or opportunity for frequent over-the-board practice, and others, having insufficient incentive to acquire book knowledge, find that their own ideas often let them down against an opponent more thoroughly grounded in general principles. There is a real problem here, in that it is hard to pay full attention to books which do not deal with the type of difficulty which occurs in one's own play. I believe the present scheme meets the difficulty in two ways: firstly, it provides a selection of games dealing with all the types of situations—positional play, attacks, sacrificial combinations, defence, and end games—which are most commonly encountered; and secondly, by inviting the reader to participate by working out the moves made by a master and commenting on his choice, it enables him to take part in a real battle against an opponent.

The book can also be taken as a collection of good games, which can be played through simply for enjoyment, without any need to answer the questions about each move. I have taken care to choose games which are, in almost all cases, from tournaments of the last few years, and which will be unfamiliar to English readers.

The more entertaining and valuable method of using the book is for the reader to imagine himself the partner of the master in the game, and to guess the moves which he makes. In this case, use a sheet of paper or card to cover each page and lower the paper line by line. The first moves of the game are given in every case, and from the diagrammed position each asterisk signifies that immediately below is a move of the side the reader is partnering, and the paper should be lowered after this move has been worked out. A maximum of 50 points can be obtained on each game. For a proper assessment of his own chess skill, the reader is recommended to work through at least one game from each of the eight sections of the book, and to average the resulting score to a proportion of 50. After calculating your eight-game average, see how you rate on the table on page x.

I CENTRE CONTROL

Game No. 1

In this game you have White. Your consultation partner is Mikhail Botvinnik, ex-champion of the world. Your opponent is Swiss master H. Grob. The game was one of eight which Botvinnik played simultaneously with clocks, in Zurich, 1956. The first moves are 1. Kt—K B 3, Kt—K B 3; 2. P—B 4, P—Q 4; 3. P × P, Kt × P; 4. P—K 4, Kt—K B 3; 5. Kt—Q B 3, P—K 3; 6. P—Q 4, P—Q B 4.

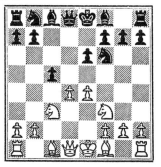

*
7. P—Q 5

4 points. Black's second move was a bad one which gave White the upper hand in the centre. The sharp 7. P—Q 5 keeps the initiative, since if now 7. ... P × P; not 8. P × P, when the isolated and easily blockaded passed pawn has little value, but 8. P—K 5, P—Q 5; 9. P × Kt, P × Kt; 10.

B—Kt 5 ch, Kt—B 3; 11. Q—K 2 ch, B—K 3; 12. O—O, Q × P; 13. B—Kt 5, which gives White a splendid game for the sacrificed pawn. 1 point each for the calmer alternatives 7. B—Q B 4, 7. B—K B 4, 7. B—Kt 5, and 7. B—K 2, but nothing for 7. B—K 3 owing to the annoying 7. ... Kt—Kt 5.

7. ...   P—Q R 3
*
8. B—Kt 5

2 points. This contains the powerful threat of 9. P—K 5, and if in reply 8. ... P—R 3; 9. B—R 4, P—K Kt 4; 10. B—Kt 3, Black's pawn position is ruined. Nothing for the tempting 8. P—Q 6 (8. ... Q × P; 9. Q × Q, B × Q; 10. P—K 5), because of the equalizing answer 8. ... P—K 4; 9. Kt × P, B × P. 1 point for the tamer 8. B—K B 4 or 8. B—K 2.

8. ...   Q—Kt 3
*
9. B × Kt

2 points. With the centre half open and the queen's side pawns already dislocated, this break-up of the king's side at once makes it impossible for Black's king to find a comfortable haven anywhere.

9. ...   P × B

1

*

10. Q—Q 2

2 points. 1 point for 10. Q—B 2 when Black's K B obtains some scope by 10. ... B—R 3.

10. ...   P—K R 4

*

11. B—K 2

1 point.

11. ...   Kt—Q 2

*

12. O—O

3 points. There is no need to fear the open K Kt file, for Black cannot hope to organize a reasonable attack with his heavy pieces necessarily split up through the unfortunate position of his king. 1 point for 12. R—Q 1, but deduct 6 points for 12. O—O—O??, B—R 3.

12. ...   P—R 5

*

13. P—R 4

3 points. The further advance of this pawn to Q R 5 will artificially isolate Black's Q B P and make it an object of attack. 1 point for 13. P—K R 3, although Black can hardly go in for 13. ... P—R 6; 14. P—K Kt 3 at present, since this would deprive his K B of the square K B 5, from where Black hopes it will simultaneously put a little pressure on White's K and also guard the weak Q-side black squares, and thus enable Black to castle Q R.

13. ...   B—R 3

*

14. Q—B 2

1 point.

14. ...   B—B 5

15. P—R 5

1 point.

15. ...   Q—B 2

*

16. K R—Q 1

1 point. White can continue quietly to improve his position, since Black's pawn weaknesses are permanent and therefore do not require to be attacked in a hurry.

16. ...   Kt—K 4

*

17. Kt × Kt

1 point.

17. ...   B × Kt

*

18. P—R 3

1 point. This is now at last necessary.

18. ...   B—Q 2

*

19. Kt—R 4

3 points. White's development is complete, so he can now go over to the attack. Before playing this move, however, White needed to foresee the variation 19. ... Q × P; 20. Kt × P, Q—B 2; 21. P × P, B × K P; 22. Q—R 4 ch, Q—B 3; 23. B—Kt 5!

19. ...   B × Kt

*

20. R × B

2 points. With the nasty threat of R—B 4, and P—Q Kt 4, this

is still stronger than 20. Q × B ch (1 point).

20. ...   R—Q B 1

*

21. R—B 4

1 point.

21. ...   Q × P

*

22. P—Q Kt 4

2 points.

22. ...   Q—R 6

*

23. R × P

3 points. 23. Kt P × P (2 points) is good, too, but the text begins a decisive break-through.

23. ...   R—Q 1

If 23. ... R × R; 24. Q × R (threat 25. Q—QB 8 ch), Q—QB 6; 25. Q × Q, B × Q; 26. R—Q B 1, winning a piece.

*

24. P × P

2 points. The black king is now exposed to the full blast of White's heavy pieces. Nothing for 24. R—B 8, when Black can hold on by 24. ... O—O.

24. ...   B—Q 3

*

25. R × B

5 points. An attractive finish, which leads to a forced win. 2 points each for 25. R—B 8 and 25. P × P ch, which win more slowly.

25. ...   R × R

*

26. R—B 8 ch

2 points.

26. ...   K—K 2

Or 26. ... R—Q 1; 27. Q—B 7, R × R; 28. Q—Q 7 ch, followed by mate.

*

27. Q—B 7 ch

2 points. 27. R × R (1 point) can of course be played, but this is more artistic.

27. ...   K × P

*

28. B—Kt 4 ch

1 point.

28. ...   P—B 4

*

29. B × P ch

1 point.

29. ...   K—K 4

*

30. Q—B 5 ch

4 points. 1 point only for 30. R × R or 30. Q—K 7 ch, R—K 3.

Black resigns.

Summary: If you made a bad score in this game, it may show one of two things. If your points were lost in the first half of the game, the implication is that you make over-hasty attacks before completing your development. If you dropped points in the second half, however, it probably means that you are not sufficiently careful in your calculations.

3

Game No. 2

In this game you have Black. Your consultation partner is Alexander Kotov, for many years one of the leading Russian grandmasters. Your opponent is A. Mangini of Brazil. The game was played at Mar del Plata, 1957.

The first moves are 1. P—K 4, P—Q B 4; 2. Kt—K B 3, P—Q 3; 3. P—Q 4, P × P; 4. Kt × P, Kt—K B 3; 5. B—Q 3, Kt—B 3; 6. P—Q B 3.

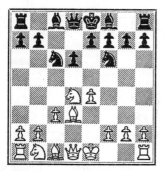

*

6. ...   P—K 4

3 points for this move, by which Black refutes his opponent's passive opening by himself advancing both central pawns. Nothing for 6. ... Kt × Kt; 7. P × Kt, which gives White two central pawns abreast; and nothing for 6. ... P—Q 4; 7. Kt × Kt, P × Kt; 8. P—K 5, when Black is driven back. 1 point for 6. ... P—K 3; or 6. ... P—K Kt 3.

7. Kt—B 2

*

7. ...   P—Q 4

2 points. Other moves allow White to build up a strong centre by P—Q B 4.

8. P × P

*

8. ...   Kt × P

1 point. Nothing for 8. ... Q × P; 9. O—O, and Black's queen is soon driven back by P—Q B 4.

9. O—O

*

9. ...   B—K 3

1 point for this or 9. ... B—Q 3. 9. ... B—K 2 is unnecessarily passive here.

10. Q—B 3

*

10. ...   B—Q 3

1 point.

11. Kt—K 3

*

11. ...   Kt × Kt

2 points. This is soundest, since if Black's attacked knight retreats, White's knight can come to the strong square K B 5, while if 11. ... Kt—B 5; 12. B—K 4, Black's knight cannot maintain its advanced post for long.

12. B × Kt

*

12. ...   O—O

1 point.

13. Kt—Q 2

4

*
13. ... P—B 4

3 points. With this move Black definitely takes the initiative. Other possibilities are more passive and allow White to improve his own position by B—K B 5 or Kt—K 4.

14. B—Q B 4

*
14. ... Q—K 2

2 points. This is again clearly better than 14. ... B × B; Black permits exchanges, but exacts as his price the constant improvement of the activity of his remaining pieces.

15. B × B ch

*
15. ... Q × B

1 point.

16. P—Q Kt 4

*
16. ... P—K 5

3 points. 16. ... P—B 5; is less good, since after 17. B—B 5, White can occupy his K 4 square with the knight and Black's attack then becomes bogged down. A strong alternative, however, is for Black to begin an attack by 16. ... R—B 3; (2 points) intending ... R —K Kt 3. 16. ... Q R—K 1 is less clear since, after 17. P—Kt 5, Black has to sacrifice his Q R P. Pawn sacrifices should be made only when there is no more certain way of making progress.

17. Q—K 2

*
17. ... Q—K 4

3 points. Not only threatening mate, but also the Q B P; this double attack entices White's pieces on to worse squares. Many players would continue 17. ...P— B 5 (no credit); but the central pawn mass cannot be turned to account so quickly; 18. B—B 5, B × B; 19. P × B, K R—K 1; 20. K R—K 1, P—K 6; 21. P × P, P × P; 22. Kt—B 1, and Black's K P is suddenly weak.

18. Q—B 4 ch

*
18. ... K—R 1

1 point.

19. P—Kt 3

*
19. ... Q R—B 1

2 points. Now White not only has a weak king's position, but his Q B P is also under heavy attack. The main threat is 20. ... Kt × P. An ingenious possibility here is 19....P—B 5; but after 20. B × B P, R × B; 21. P × R, Q × K B P; 22. K R—Q 1, Q × R P ch; 23. K—B 1, P—K 6; 24. Kt—K 4, Black's attack does not appear quite sufficient. When, as here, your advantage is of an enduring type (weak enemy pawns and squares) you can afford to strengthen your position to the maximum degree before beginning the final assault.

20. K R—Q 1

5

*
20. ...　　　　Q—B 3

4 points. White's last move baited a trap: if 20. ... Kt × P; 21. P × Kt, R × Q; 22. Kt × R, followed by Kt × B, and White has more than sufficient material for the queen. Now, however, Black threatens ... Kt—K 4—Q 6.

21. Q—Kt 3

*
21. ...　　　　B—K 4

2 points. Clearer than 21. ... Kt —K 4 (1 point), when White could still confuse the situation by 22. B—Q 4 or 22. B × P. Now White's weak Q B P is fixed as a target.

22. Kt—B 4

*
22. ...　　　　P—B 5

4 points. 2 points for 22. ... B × B P; which should also win (23. R—Q 6, B × R; 24. R × Q, B × R; 25. Kt—Q 6, R—Q B 2). The text, however, is much sharper, for if 23. B × B P, B × B; 24. P × B, Q × K B P; followed by ... P—Q Kt 4 and Kt—K 4; Black clearly has a decisive attack, while if 23. Kt × B, P × B.

23. B—B 5

*
23. ...　　　　P—K 6

4 points. Again much sharper than 23. ... B × P or 23. ... K R —K 1 (1 point each). Black's strategy follows a pattern which Alekhine employed in some of his most sensational wins; the opponent's forces are diverted to the defence of a weakness on one wing, and this enables the attacker to make a decisive thrust on the other side of the board.

24. B × R

(If 24. P × K P, P × Kt P wins quickly, as does 24. P × B P, Q × P; or 24. Kt × B, P × P ch).

*
24. ...　　　　P × P ch

3 points. Simply 24. ... R × B (3 points) is also very good, but not 24. ... P × Kt P (no credit); 25. B P × Kt P!

25. K—Kt 2

(Or 25. K × P, P × P db. ch.).

*
25. ...　　　　R × B

2 points. Deduct 2 points for 25. ... P × P; 26. B—B 5, when there is no mate in sight, and no credit for 25. ... P—B 6 ch; 26. K × P.

26. R—Q 3

*
26. ...　　　　P × P

2 points. If now 27. P × P, P— B 8(Q) ch.

27. Kt—Q 2

*
27. ...　　　　P × P

1 point.

28. Kt—B 1

*
28. ...　　　　Q—Kt 3 ch

2 points.

6

White resigns, for after 29. R—
Kt 3, B × R; 30. Kt × B, P—
B 8(Q) ch; 31. R × Q, R × R;
32. K × R, Q × Kt; the game is
over.

Summary: Readers who have
made a bad score in this game will
probably find that they have fallen
into one of two traps: either they
over-pressed their attack early in
the game, before Black had enough
pieces developed to support his
central advance, or else they were
too cautious later on, underestimating the greatly enhanced
value of Black's pieces after the
pawns were thrust forward and
lines opened for the attack.

II SUPERIOR DEVELOPMENT

Game No. 3

IN this game you have Black. Your consultation partner is the author. Your opponent is the noted London player A. Y. Green. The game was played at Bognor, 1956.
The first moves are 1. P—Q 4, Kt—K B 3; 2. P—Q B 4, P—K Kt 3; 3. P—K Kt 3, B—Kt 2; 4. B—Kt 2, O—O; 5. Kt—K B 3, P—Q 3; 6. O—O, Kt—B 3; 7. P—Q 5, Kt—Q R 4; 8. K Kt—Q 2, P—B 3; 9. Kt—Q B 3, P × P; 10. P × P.

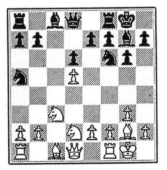

*

| 10. ... | Kt—Kt 5 |

2 points. White was threatening 11. P—Q Kt 4, Kt—Kt 5; 12. B—Kt 2, winning a piece, but this could be more economically prevented by simply 10. ... B—Q 2 (3 points); and if 11. P—Q Kt 4, R—B 1. I aimed to occupy K 4

with my knight, but it is not completely secure on that square.

| 11. R—Kt 1 |

*

| 11. ... | B—Q 2 |

2 points. Black, of course, does not occupy K 4 until White has lost a tempo with P—K R 3.

| 12. P—K R 3 |

*

| 12. ... | Kt—K 4 |

1 point.

| 13. P—Kt 3 |

*

| 13. ... | Q—B 1 |

3 points. White's last move was an oversight of which Black takes immediate advantage.

| 14. P—Q Kt 4 |

*

| 14. ... | Kt(R 4)—B 5 |

4 points. When in doubt, it is usually better to choose a line ensuring a permanent positional advantage than one involving doubtful complications. Here, for example, 14. ... Q × Kt (1 point); 15. P × Kt would lead to a wild game by 15. ... Q × R P; 16. R × P threatening 17 P—B 4, or 15. ... Q R—Kt 1; 16. B—Kt 2, Q × R P; 17. P—B 4.

| 15. K—R 2 |

*

15. ...   Kt × Kt

2 points. 15. ... Kt—K 6 (2 points); 16. P × Kt, Q × Kt; was also strong, as was the quiet 15. ... P—Q Kt 4 (2 points). By the text-move, however, Black envisaged a forced line of play resulting in occupation of the seventh rank.

16. Q × Kt

*

16. ...   B—B 4

2 points for this, 16. ... Kt—B 5; or 16. ... Kt—Kt 5 ch. Black baits a trap, for the obvious 17. P—K 4 now fails to 17. ... B × R P!

17. Kt—K 4

*

17. ...   Q—B 5

3 points. Black simultaneously invades along the Q B file and shuts out White's K B, for if now 18. Q—K 3, Black can simply capture the Q R P.

18. P—B 3

*

18. ...   K R—B 1

2 points. In the circumstances, slightly better than 18 .... Q R—B 1 (1 point) since Black may wish to open the Q R file later.

19. R—Q 1

*

19. ...   Q—B 7

2 points.

20. R—Kt 2

*

20. ...   Q—R 5

3 points. Black threatens 21. ... Kt—B 5; and prepares for a

second attack on the seventh rank by ... R—B 2; ... Q R—B 1; and ... R—B 7.

21. Q—K 1

*

21. ...   R—B 2

2 points. 21. ... Kt—B 5 (2 points) was also very strong.

22. Kt—Q 2

*

22. ...   B—B 7

2 points. White's last move was a blunder, of course, but his position was in any case extremely difficult.

23. Kt—Kt 3

*

23. ...   B × R

1 point.

24. Q × B

*

24. ...   Q R—Q B 1

3 points. Stronger than 24. ... Q × Kt P (1 point); the threat is 25. ... R × B.

25. R—Q 2

*

25. ...   Q × Kt P

1 point.

26. P—K R 4

*

26. ...   P—Q R 4

4 points. Now White cannot avoid further material loss.

27. P—R 3

9

* 27. ...   Q—Kt 3

2 points. 1 point for 27. ...Q—Kt 4; 28. Kt—Q 4, and White can hold on a little longer.

28. P—R 4

* 28. ...   R—B 6

4 points.

29. B—K R 3

* 29. ...   R (B 1)—B 2

2 points.

30. P—B 4

* 30. ...   Q × Kt

Winning another piece (1 point). White resigns.

Summary: White's difficulties arose from his not taking sufficient notice of the dangers arising from an unguarded piece (move 13).

Many games which are lost by tactical blunders of this kind would be saved if the player took the precaution, before making EVERY move, of taking a quick look round the board for any tactical possibilities present (*a*) in the position as it stands, and (*b*) in the position which will occur after he has moved. I cannot emphasize too much the value of this advice for any readers who find that they are liable to be caught by traps and elementary combinations.

The second point to notice about this game is the way in which Black, with a clear and permanent strategical advantage, refused to be diverted into scrappy positions where White might obtain counter-chances (Black's 14th and 15th). If you chose differently on these two moves, it may indicate that your games lack a guiding plan and that you jump about from one idea to another.

III POSITIONAL PLAY

Game No. 4

In this game you have White. Your consultation partner is German grandmaster Wolfgang Unzicker. Your opponent is Miguel Sanchez of Colombia. The game was played in the world championship interzonal tournament at Saltsjobaden, Sweden, 1952. The first moves are 1. P—K 4, P—K 4; 2. Kt—K B 3, Kt—Q B 3; 3. B—Kt 5, P—Q R 3; 4. B—R 4, Kt—B 3; 5. O—O, B—K 2; 6. R—K 1, P—Q Kt 4; 7. B—Kt 3, P—Q 3; 8. P—B 3, Kt—Q R 4; 9. B—B 2, P—B 4; 10. P—Q 4, Q—B 2; 11. P—Q R 4, P—Kt 5; 12. B P × P, P × Kt P; 13. P—R 3, O—O; 14. Q Kt—Q 2, B—Q 2; 15. Kt—B 1, K R —B 1.

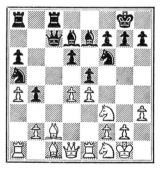

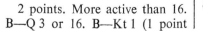

16. Kt—K 3

2 points. More active than 16. B—Q 3 or 16. B—Kt 1 (1 point each); in the Ruy Lopez White's Q Kt usually aims to reach Q 5 or K B 5.

16. ...   Kt—B 3

*

17. B—Kt 3

3 points. Black threatened to win a pawn by 17. ... Kt × Q P (deduct 3 points if you overlooked this). 17 P—Q 5 (no credit) is rarely good in such positions, since it abandons the attempt to make Black capture on White's Q 4 and also takes away a good square from the white knights; while 17. P × P (no credit) is also innocuous. So White moves his bishop back to a good diagonal. The reply 17. ... K Kt × P? fails to 18. Kt—Q 5.

17. ...   Kt—Q R 4

*

18. B—Q 5

2 points. This is much stronger than repeating moves by 18. B— B 2 (1 point) or than 18. Kt—Q 5 (1 point).

18. ...   B—B 3

*

19. B × B

2 points. White's advantage would disappear if Black were allowed to exchange twice on his Q 4.

19. ...   Kt × B

11

*

20. Kt—B 5

3 points. Now the knight is happily established on one of its two 'ideal' outposts.

20. ...   B—B 1

*

21. B—Kt 5

2 points. Developing and threatening at the same time, for Black cannot afford to let White permanently secure his knight's position by 22. B × Kt.

21. ...   Kt—K 1

*

22. R—Q B 1

1 point.

22. ...   Q—Kt 2

*

23. Q—Q 3

3 points. White has satisfactorily established his advantage in the centre and on the king's side, and now must look for a new means of attack. There is nothing further to be done on the king's side for the moment, since the black pawn wall is unbroken and he has two minor pieces handy to defend his king. However, Black's Q Kt P can be easily attacked and if it is safeguarded by ... P—Q R 4 White will have another outpost available for occupation at Q Kt 5. 23. Q—Kt 3 and 23. R—B 4 (same idea) are met by 23. ... Kt—R 4.

23. ...   R—B 2

*

24. Kt—K 3

3 points. Now that Black's K Kt and K B are passively posted, this knight can join in the Q-side offensive; after Black's last move it can reach Q 5 with gain of time.

24. ...   Q R—B 1

*

25. Kt—Q 5

1 point.

25. ...   R—Q 2

*

26. B—Q 2

2 points. The logical move to increase the pressure on the Q Kt P.

26. ...   P—Kt 3

*

27. R—B 4

2 points. Now Black can scarcely protect his Q Kt P, for after 27. ... P—Q R 4; follows 28. K R—Q B 1, with a crippling pin on the Q B file.

27. ...   P × P

*

28. B × P

3 points. Much better than 28. Kt × Kt P; the knight at Q 5 is a tower of strength and should not be exchanged. Deduct 4 points for 28. Kt × Q P?, Kt—K 4.

28. ...   B—Kt 2

*

29. B—Q 2

6 points. The idea of this fine move is that after 29 K R—Q B 1 (no credit), Black could still save himself by 29. ... Kt × B! Now, however, 30. K R—Q B 1 is a terrible threat, e.g. 29. ... Q × P; 30. K R—Q B 1, Q—Kt 2; 31.

R—Kt 1, Q—R 2; 32. Kt—Kt 6, and wins, or 29. ... Kt—K 4; 30. Kt × Kt, P × Kt; 31. R × R, Q × R; 32. Kt—Kt 6.

29. ...   R—Kt 1

*

30. K R—Q B 1

1 point.

30. ...   Kt—K 4

*

31. Kt × Kt

1 point.

31. ...   P × Kt

*

32. R—Kt 4

4 points. This wins a pawn immediately. 32. Q—B 2 (3 points) is strong too.

32. ...   Q—R 2

*

33. R × R

2 points.

33. ...   Q × R

*

34. Q × R P

1 point.

34. ...   R—Kt 2

If 34. ... Q × P; 35. R—B 8, Q × B; 36. R × Kt ch, B—B 1; 37. Kt—B 6 ch.

*

35. R—B 8

6 points. A crushing finish, after which Black resigns. If 35 ... Q × R; 36. Kt—K 7 ch.

Summary: Note how White's persistent initiative was due to his use of the central squares Q 5 and K B 5 as jumping-off points for his minor pieces (moves 18, 20, and 25). Another factor in White's win was his use of the 'alternation' principle. Black's minor pieces were driven into defensive positions (moves 20 and 21) and then White used his superior mobility to transfer the attack to the other wing, where he was thus able to have a decisive superiority of force available (moves 24-27).

13

Game No. 5

IN this game you have Black. Your consultation partner is Julio Bolbochan, the Argentinian, who has the reputation of being the hardest player in the world to defeat. Your opponent is G. Idigoras. The game was played at Mar del Plata, 1956.

The first moves are 1. P—Q 4, Kt—K B 3; 2. P—Q B 4, P—K Kt 3; 3. P—K Kt 3, B—Kt 2; 4. B—Kt 2, O—O; 5. Kt—K B 3, P—Q 3; 6. O—O, Kt—B 3; 7. P—Kt 3, R—Kt 1; 8. B—Kt 2, P—Q R 3; 9. P—Q 5, Kt—Q R 4; 10. Kt—Q 4, B—Q 2; 11. Kt—Q 2, P—B 4; 12. P × P e.p., P × P; 13. R—Kt 1.

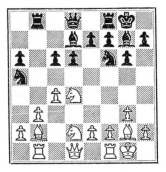

*

13. ...   P—B 4

2 points. Black's advantage here is very slight. He has the majority of pawns in the centre, but they can scarcely be advanced without creating weaknesses. White has no weak points, although Black may be able to obtain pressure later on by massing his heavy pieces on the Q Kt file and advancing his Q R P.

On the other hand, it is very hard for White to find any constructive plan, for his prospects of initiative on either wing are greatly diminished by Black's hold on the centre, which he strengthens by 13. ... P—B 4. Nothing for 13. ... P—K 4; 14. Kt (Q 4)—B 3, when Black's Q P is a weakness.

14. Kt—B 2

*

14. ...   Q—B 1

2 points. The exchange of White's K B is necessary if Black is to operate on the Q Kt file. Reasonable alternatives, although less thematic, are 14. ... B—B 3; and 14. ... Kt—B 3.

15. Kt—K 3

*

15. ...   Kt—B 3

2 points. Nothing for the immediate 15. ... B—R 6; when 16. B × Kt, K B × B; 17. Kt—Q 5! is rather awkward—hence Black guards the K P, simultaneously re-centralizing the knight.

16. Kt—Q 5

*

16. ...   Kt × Kt

1 point.

17. P × Kt

*

17. ...   Kt—K 4

2 points. A little better than 17. ... Kt—Q 5 (1 point) since the knight is then at once driven from its centralized post by 18. P—K 3

14

or 18. Kt—B 3. Deduct 6 points for the blunder 17. ... B × B?; 18 P × Kt, winning a piece. After 17. ... Kt—K 4; 18. P—B 4, Kt—Kt 5; is obviously bad for White.

18. Q—B 2

*

18. ...   B—R 6

1 point.

19. Kt—B 4

*

19. ...   B × B

1 point.

20. K × B

*

20. ...   Kt × Kt

1 point. Another necessary exchange, since after 20. ... Kt—Q 2 (no credit); White's knight is too well posted, and otherwise White simply doubles and isolates his opponent's pawns by 21. Kt × Kt.

21. P × Kt

*

21. ...   B × B

1 point.

22. R × B

*

22. ...   R × R

2 points. Against other moves the reply is 23 K R—Q Kt 1, and White's assured possession of the Q Kt file is a useful asset.

23. Q × R

*

23. ...   Q—Kt 5

2 points. Now we can see why Black's advantage persists, despite the exchanges. This type of pawn formation often results from King's Indian Defence type of openings where Black plays ... P—Q B 4. The weakness in White's position lies in the fact that the base of his pawn chain at Q B 4 is vulnerable to attack, while Black's base at K 2 is much more easily defended. Deduct a point for the unimaginative 23. ... Q—B 2 and 23. ... Q—Kt 1; both answered by 24. R—Q Kt 1.

24. Q—B 2

*

24. ...   R—Kt 1

1 point.

25. P—K 4

*

25. ...   P—Q R 4

3 points. This threatens 26. ... P—R 5; 27. Q × P (else 27. ... P—R 6;), Q × K P ch; followed by ... R—Kt 5; winning a pawn.

26. P—K R 3

*

26. ...   Q—R 4

3 points. Now the threat is 27. ... P—R 5; 28. Q × P, Q—K 7.

27. P—B 3

*

27. ...   Q—K 4

2 points. Finally White is forced to exchange rooks, but the queen and pawn ending also has its troubles.

28. R—Q Kt 1

*

28. ...   R × R

1 point.

29. Q × R

15

*
29. ...   P—R 5
3 points. Black cannot be prevented from completing his plan, for if 30. P—R 3, Q—B 6; 31. Q—R 2, Q—Kt 6.
30. Q—B 2
*
30. ...   P—R 6
1 point.
31. Q—K 2
*
31. ...   P—Kt 4
5 points for this or 31. ... P—R 4. There is nothing more to be done on the queen's side for the moment (no credit for 31. ...Q—Kt 7; 32. K—B 2), so Black creates an entry point on the opposite wing.
32. K—B 2
*
32. ...   P—R 4
1 point.
33. Q—Q 2
*
33. ...   P—R 5
2 points.
34. P × P
*
34. ...   P × P
1 point.
35. K—B 1
*
35. ...   K—B 1
2 points. Deduct 6 points for 35. ... Q—Kt 6?; 36. Q—K Kt 2, when Black may even lose the pawn ending.
36. K—K 2
*
36. ...   K—K 1
2 points.
37. K—K 3

*
37. ...   P—B 4
2 points. Black is intent on obtaining the maximum possible positional advantage before transposing into a pawn ending.
38. Q—Q B 2
*
38. ...   K—B 2
2 points for this or 38 ... P—B 5 ch.
39. Q—Q 3
*
39. ...   P—B 5 ch
1 point.
40. K—B 2
*
40. ...   Q—Kt 7 ch
1 point. White resigns, for after 41. Q—K 2, K—B 3; 42. K—B 1, K—K 4; 43. Q—Q 3, Q—R 8 ch; 44. K—K 2, Q × P ch; followed by 45. ... Q—Q Kt 7; Black wins with ease.

Summary: Where strong players are concerned, it is often very difficult to make any impression with the black pieces, but in such a case the experienced master will play on and accumulate such positional advantages as he can. If you obtained a bad score in this game, it could mean that you were not sufficiently aware that Black had an advantage at all. If you are prone to draw a large number of your games, the moral should be clear.

Game No. 6

IN this game you have Black. Your consultation partner is V. Suetin of the U.S.S.R. Your opponent is Monillaux of France. The game was played in the Students' World Team Championship in Lyons, 1955. The first moves are 1. P—K 4, P—Q B 4; 2. Kt—K B 3, P—Q 3; 3. B—K 2, Kt—K B 3; 4. Kt—B 3, Kt—B 3; 5. P—Q 4, P × P; 6. Kt × P, P—K 4; 7. Kt—Kt 3, B—K 2; 8. O—O, O—O; 9. B—K 3, P—Q R 4; 10. P—Q R 4.

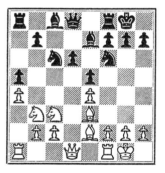

*

10. ...   Kt—Q Kt 5

3 points. Boleslavsky's variation of the Sicilian is nowadays one of the most popular of all, for experience has shown that Black's backward Q P involves no difficulties. By inducing White to play P—Q R 4 on the last move, Black made it possible for himself to post his Q Kt on this strong square where it supports the coming ... P—Q 4; and ties down the white queen to defence. 3

points for 10. ... B—K 3; which is equally strong.

11. P—B 4

*

11. ...   B—K 3

1 point for this, but 3 points for the more accurate 11. ... P × P; 12. B × P, B—K 3; threatening both 13. ... P—Q 4; and 13. ... Kt × B P! (14. Q × Kt, Q—Kt 3 ch).

12. P—B 5

*

12. ...   B—Q 2

2 points. Nothing for 12. ... B—B 1 or 12. ... B × Kt; the B must support the advance of the Q P.

13. B—B 3

*

13. ...   B—B 3

1 point.

14. B—Kt 5

(Better 14 Q—K 2, followed by Q R—Q 1, so as to make Black submit to a pin on the Q file as the price of carrying through ... P—Q 4).

*

14. ...   Q—B 2

2 points.

15. B × Kt

*

15. ...   B × B

1 point.

16. Q—K 2

*

16. ...   QR—Q1

2 points for this or 16. ...K R
—Q 1.

17. QR—Q1

*

17. ...   R—Q2

3 points. This saves a move over
17. ... P—Q Kt 3 (1 point).

18. K—R 1

*

18. ...   KR—Q1

1 point.

19. Kt—B 1

*

19. ...   P—Q4

3 points. Of course! No further
preparation is needed.

20. P × P

*

20. ...   Kt × Q P

1 point.

21. Kt × Kt

*

21. ...   B × Kt

1 point.

22. B × B

*

22. ...   R × B

1 point.

23. R × R

*

23. ...   R × R

1 point.

24. R—Q 1

*

24. ...   R × R ch

2 points for this or for 24. ...
Q—Q 1, Q 2, or Q 3, which are
also excellent.

25. Q × R

*

25. ...   P—R 3

2 points. Nothing for the impatient 25. ... Q—Q 1; 26. Q ×
Q ch, B × Q; 27. Kt—Q 3, P—
B 3; 28. Kt—B 5, when the win,
if possible, is very difficult.

26. Kt—K 2

*

26. ...   P—K 5

3 points. If now 27. P—B 3,
Q—Q B 5; followed by ... Q—Q 6,
when White is at a loss for reasonable moves.

27. Kt—Kt 3

*

27. ...   B × P

2 points.

28. Kt × P

*

28. ...   Q—K B 5

3 points. 28. ... Q—Q B 5 (2
points) is also sufficient.

29. Kt—B 5

*

29. ...   B—K 4

3 points.

30. P—Kt 3

*

30. ...   Q—B 5

3 points for this, and 1 point for
30. ... Q × B P; 31. Q—Q 8 ch,

K—R 2; 32. Q—Q 3, when Black
still has some technical difficulties.

31. Kt—Q 3

*
31. ...   Q—Q 4 ch

2 points.

32. K—Kt 1

*
32. ...   B—Q 5 ch

1 point.

33. K—B 1

Not 33 Kt—B 2, B × Kt ch;
which explains why Black preferred ... Q—Q 4 ch to ... Q—
K 5 ch on move 31.

*
33. ...   Q—R 8 ch

3 points. 1 only for 33. ...Q ×
P ch.
White resigns, for if 34. K—K 2,
Q—Kt 7 ch; 35. K—K 1, B—
B 6 ch.

Summary: This game can really
be divided into two parts: the first,
up to move 19, where Black
devotes all his energies to realiz-
ing the advance ... P—Q 4—if you
did badly here it means you should
check up, before playing any
move, to make sure that it has a
part in your plan of action. The
second half of the game, from
move 24 to the end, is a test of a
player's ability to evaluate a
positional advantage in the most
accurate way.

19

Game No. 7

In this game you have Black. Your consultation partner is the Franco-Polish master Stephan Popel, who is now living in the U.S.A. Your opponent is one of Britain's most promising young players, B. J. Moore. The game was played in the Premier Reserves Major tournament at Hastings, 1955-6.

The first moves are 1. P—Q 4, Kt—K B 3; 2. Kt—K B 3, P—K 3; 3. P—B 4, B—Kt 5 ch; 4. B—Q 2, Q—K 2; 5. P—K 3, O—O; 6. B—Q 3, Kt—B 3; 7. P—Q R 3, B × B ch; 8. Q Kt × B, P—Q 3; 9. O—O, P—K 4; 10. P—Q 5, Kt—Kt 1; 11. P—K 4.

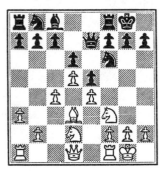

*

11. ...   B—Kt 5

2 points. In this blocked position the bishops, particularly White's, have little scope; Black can therefore allow the exchange of his own bishop for a knight so as to increase his own knight's chances of occupying the black squares Q B 4, Q 5 and K B 5. 1 point each for 11. ...P—Q R 4;

and 11. ... P—Q B 4; which are quite playable.

12. Q—B 2

*

12. ...   Q Kt—Q 2

1 point for this or 12. ...P—Q R 4.

13. P—Q Kt 4

*

13. ...   P—Q R 4

1 point.

14. K R—B 1

*

14. ...   P × P

2 points. Opening the Q R file in itself has no particular strength; but Black has an interesting plan for fixing his opponent's queen's side, which reveals itself in the next few moves. 2 points for 14. ... K R—B 1, another good positional move which prepares ... Kt B 1-Kt 3—B 5 and also ... P—Q B 3.

15. P × P

*

15. ...   P—B 4

2 points. The reply is forced, for 16. P × P, Kt × B P; or, 16. P—Kt 5, Kt—Kt 3; makes White's bishop a very helpless piece indeed.

16. P × P e.p.

*

16. ...   P × P

1 point.

20

17. Kt—K 1

Preferable and more active is 17. R × R, R × R; 18. P—B 5.

*

17. ...   P—B 4

2 points. Now Black's manœuvre to fix the queen's side is complete. The outside passed pawn is of no great importance, since it cannot advance for a long time to come.

18. P—Kt 5

*

18. ...   Kt—Kt 3

1 point.

19. Kt—B 1

*

19. ...   Q—Kt 2

3 points. A multi-purpose move: it guards against R—R 6, prepares in some eventualities the exchange of the rooks on the Q R file and its occupation by the queen, and keeps an eye on the white K P.

20. Kt—K 3

*

20. ...   P—Kt 3

2 points. It is more logical to keep the K P fixed rather than permit 20. ... B—K 3 (1 point); 21. Kt—B 5, B × Kt; 22. P × B, although in that case, too, Black would retain some advantage.

21. Kt × B

*

21. ...   Kt × Kt

1 point.

22. B—K 2

*

22. ...   Kt—B 3

2 points. Nothing for 22. ... P—B 4; when White's feeble bishop is able to obtain some scope by 23 P × P, P × P; 24. Q—Q 2, with B—B 3 in the offing.

23. B—B 3

*

23. ...   R × R

1 point. Exchanges normally accentuate the handicap which a player suffers from having a strategically useless piece, as White's bishop is here.

24. R × R

*

24. ...   R—R 1

1 point.

25. R—Q 1

*

25. ...   Kt—K 1

2 points. How should Black protect the attacked Q P? The queen and rook are clearly intended for an invasion along the Q R file, while the knight at Q Kt 3, besides blockading the Q Kt P, attacks the Q B P, which will be the first target of Black's invasion.

26. B—K 2

*

26. ...   R—R 5

2 points. 1 point for 26. ... R—R 4; or 26. ... R—R 6

27. P—B 3

*
27. ...   Q—R 1
1 point for this or 27. ... Q—R 2.
28. R—Q 2

*
28. ...   Q—R 4
2 points. 1 point for 28. ... R—R 8.
29. K—B 2

*
29. ...   K—B 1
1 point. Black, it seems, cannot improve his position for the moment and so centralizes his king in readiness for the ending.
30. P—Kt 3

*
30. ...   K—K 2
1 point.
31. Kt—Kt 2

*
31. ...   Kt × P
4 points, and 4 points if you chose this on either of the two previous moves, when it was equally playable.
32. B × Kt

*
32. ...   R × B
1 point.
33. Q × R

*
33. ...   Q × R ch
1 point.
34. K—B 1

*
34. ...   Q—Q 8 ch
1 point. Now the knight is tied down, for if 35. K—B 2, Q—Q 5 ch.
35. Kt—K 1

*
35. ...   Q—Kt 8
1 point.
36. Q—R 4

*
36. ...   Kt—B 2
2 points. White resigns. With the loss of a second pawn, his game is hopeless.

Summary: The theme of Black's excellent positional play here is the reducing of White's bishop to helplessness. Black steadily (moves 11, 13, 15, 18) consolidates his hold on the black squares and ties down this bishop to purely passive defence, and only then invades along the Q R file. Many players are too prone to attack before firmly establishing what positional advantages are inherent in their position, and for them this game should be a valuable corrective.

Game No. 8

In this game you have White. Your consultation partner is Czechoslovakia's leading player, Dr. Miroslav Filip. Your opponent is Jan Sefc. The game was played in the international tournament at Marianske Lazne, 1956. The first moves are 1. P—Q B 4, P—K 3; 2. P—K Kt 3, P—Q 4; 3. B—Kt 2, P × P; 4. Q—R 4 ch, B—Q 2; 5. Q × B P, B—B 3; 6. Kt—K B 3, Kt—Q 2; 7. O—O, K Kt —B 3; 8. Q—B 2, P—K 4; 9. Kt—B 3, B—Q 3; 10. P—K 4, B—B 4; 11. R—Q 1, Kt—Kt 5; 12. R—B 1, O—O; 13. P—K R 3, K Kt—B 3; 14. R—Q 1, Q—K 2.

*
15. P—Q 4

4 points. White's advantage here consists of the centre majority of pawns and in the awkward positioning of his opponent's bishops.

15. ...   P × P

*
16. Kt × P

1 point.

16. ...   B × Kt

*
17. R × B

1 point.

17. ...   K R—K 1

*
18. P—Q Kt 4

4 points. The minority attack is particularly effective here, since Black's bishop is a vulnerable target.

18. ...   P—Q R 3

*
19. B—B 4

3 points for this, 2 for 19. P— Q R 4, and 4 points if you chose 18 B—B 4 last move.

19. ...   Kt—K 4

*
20. Q R—Q 1

2 points. This is one of the positions where very simple moves keep the advantage. Black cannot now contest the Q file immediately owing to the loss of the knight on K 4.

20. ...   Kt—Kt 3

*
21. B—K 3

2 points. 21. B—Kt 5 (1 point), P—K R 3 is also possible, though no particular improvement.

21. ...   K R—Q 1

*
22. Q—Q 2

3 points. Again played in order to keep control of the Q file.

22. ...   R × R

23

*

23. Q × R
1 point.

23. ...   R—K 1

*

24. P—B 3
1 point.

24. ...   P—R 3

*

25. P—Q R 4

4 points. Now that the centre is under control, White can revert to the minority attack.

25. ...   P—Kt 3

*

26. B—B 2

3 points. White could also play 26. P—Kt 5 (3 points) immediately, but there is no hurry; Black's pawn weaknesses would be accentuated if he advanced ... P—Q R 4 or ... P—Q Kt 4.

26. ...   B—Kt 2

*

27. K—R 2

1 point for this or 27. P—Kt 5.

27. ...   Kt—K 4

*

28. P—Kt 5
1 point.

28. ...   P × P

*

29. P × P
1 point.

29. ...   Kt—Kt 3

*

30. Kt—K 2

6 points. The obvious target for White here is Black's Q B P; however, if White attacks it by simply transferring his queen and rook to the Q B file, Black will obtain counterplay by himself occupying the Q file. So White plans first to tie his opponent's queen to the defence of the weak pawn by P—K Kt 4 and B—Kt 3. However, the immediate 30. P—Kt 4 would be countered by 30. ... Kt—B 5—hence 30. Kt—K 2.

30. ...   Kt—B 1

*

31. Kt—B 4

4 points. Now Black threatened to free his queen from the defence of the pawn by 31. ... Kt—K 3.

31. ...   Kt—K 3

*

32. Kt × Kt
1 point.

32. ...   Q × Kt

*

33. P—Kt 4
1 point.

33. ...   Q—K 4 ch

*

34. Q × Q
1 point.

34. ...   R × Q

*

35. B—B 1

2 points. Deduct 5 points if you failed to notice that the Q Kt P was attacked.

35. ...   R—K 2

*

36. B—Kt 3
1 point.

36. ...   K—B 1

24

After this Black loses quickly, but he has already no reasonable defence to the threatened 37. R—Q 8 ch, K—R 2; 38. R—Q Kt 8, P—B 4; 39. P × P e.p., B × P; 40. R × P, when although the pawns are all on the same side of the board, White's possession of the two bishops makes the win theoretically sure.

*

37. R—Q 8 ch

1 point.

37. ...   R—K 1

A sad decision; but if 37. ... Kt—K 1; 38. R—Kt 8, P—B 3; 39. B—Q 6.

*

38. B × P

1 point. A sound pawn up, with the rooks exchanged and two bishops controlling the board, White has an easy win. The remaining moves were 38. ... R × R; 39. B × R, Kt—Q 2; 40. B—B 7, K—K 2; 41. K—Kt 3, P—Kt 4; 42. K—B 2, B—R 1; 43. K—K 3, B—Kt 2; 44. K—Q 4, P—B 3; 45. B—Q B 4, K—K 1; 46. B—Q 5, B—B 1; 47. B—B 6, K—K 2; 48. K—Q 5, Kt—K 4; 49. B—Q 6 ch, K—B 2; 50. B × Kt, Resigns.

Summary: In master play, the two bishops in a reasonably open position form virtually a winning advantage in themselves, other factors being equal. Note here how Black was steadily driven back as the bishops, operating on adjacent diagonals, controlled the whole board.

Game No. 9

In this game you have Black. Your consultation partner is Nicolas Rossolimo, the French master who is now residing in the U.S.A. Your opponent is the author. The game was played at Hastings, 1950-1.

The first moves are 1. P—K 4, P—Q B 4; 2. Kt—K B 3, P—Q 3; 3. P—Q 4, P × P; 4. Kt × P, Kt—K B 3; 5. Kt—Q B 3, P—Q R 3; 6. P—B 4, P—K 3; 7. B K 2, Q—B 2; 8. O—O, Kt—B 3; 9. B—K 3, B—Q 2; 10. P—K Kt 4 (premature before Black has castled).

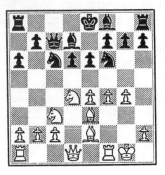

*

10. ...   Kt × Kt

2 points. Black's first concern, before he attempts anything else, must be to provide a better retreat square for his K Kt than K Kt 1. The only alternative worth considering is 10 .... O—O—O (1 point); 11. P—Kt 5, Kt—K 1; but in that case the theoretical weakness of White's having advanced his pawns on the wing where he is castled would be outweighed in practice by the enduring initiative which would result.

11. B × Kt

*

11. ...   B—B 3

1 point.

12. B—B 3

*

12. ...   P—K 4

2 points. A well-timed central attack which must lead to either the freeing of Black's K B or the splitting of White's pawns. Nothing for 12. ... P—Q 4; which would be quite good were White to reply 13. P—K 5, Kt—K 5; but which leads to trouble after 13. P × P, P × P; 14. R—K 1 ch.

13. B—K 3

*

13. ...   B—K 2

1 point. 13. ... P × P; 14. B × P, B—K 2; is not so convincing in view of the weakness of the Q P.

14. P—B 5

Better 14. P—Kt 5.

*

14. ...   P—R 3!

For after this excellent reply (3 points) White's attack is completely halted and he is left with a bad K B hemmed in by its own pawns and a number of weaknesses on the black squares. If now 15. P—Kt 5, P × P; 16. B × P, Q—Kt 3 ch; and 17. ... Q × P; is quite safe.

15. Q—Q 2

*
15. ...   P—Q Kt 4

2 points. Compare this game with No. 24. This is another of the rare occasions when it is good to retain the king in the centre and attack on the wings. Clearly 15. ... O—O? (deduct 4 points) would soon make White's attack overwhelming after 16. P—K R 4, while 15. ... O—O—O (no credit) would also give White some welcome counterplay after 16. P—Kt 4.

16. Q R—Q 1

*
16. ...   R—Q B 1

2 points. Much less accurate is 16. ... P—Kt 5 (no credit); 17. Kt—Q 5, which is now prevented owing to the loose Q B P. Also playable, however, is 16. ... Q—Kt 2; pinning White down to the defence of his K P.

17. P—Q R 3

*
17. ...   Q—Kt 2

1 point.

18. Q—Q 3

*
18. ...   Kt—Q 2

3 points. Black is aiming to create fresh pawn weaknesses as attacking targets; the knight threatens to invade at Q B 4 or Q B 5.

19. P—Kt 4

*
19. ...   Kt—Kt 3

1 point.

20. B—B 1

*
20. ...   Kt—B 5

1 point.

21. Kt—Q 5

*
21. ...   B × Kt

1 point.

22. P × B

*
22. ...   B—Kt 4

2 points. By this familiar stratagem Black exchanges off his opponent's 'good' bishop and leaves its anaemic companion hemmed in by its own pawns.

23. K R—K 1

*
23. ...   Q—K 2

2 points for this, and 1 point for 23. ... B × B.

24. B—K 4

*
24. ...   B × B

1 point.

25. R × B

*
25. ...   P—K R 4

3 points. The perfect culmination of Black's beautiful strategy —the attack, smoothly in motion on the queen's side, is transferred to the opposite wing as well. 1 point for 25. ... Q—Kt 4.

26. Q—K Kt 3

*
26. ...   P × P

2 points. Decidedly not 26. ... P—R 5? (deduct a point). Black can make good use of the open K R file.

27. Q × Kt P

*

27. ...   Q—B 3

1 point. Black prevents 28. P—
B 6.

28. B—Q 3

*

28. ...   R—R 5

1 point.

29. Q—Kt 3

*

29. ...   Kt—Kt 3

2 points. This is played not just
to attack the Q P, but to bring the
knight into the attack on the other
wing. 3 points for 29. ... Kt × P;
which is also sufficient (30. R—
R 1, Kt × P; 31. Q R—B 1, Kt ×
R; 32. R × R ch, K—Q 2).

30. R—K 4

*

30. ...   R—R 4

2 points. Nothing for 30. ...
R × R; 31. B × R, R—B 5;
32. R—K 1.

31. R—Kt 4

*

31. ...   Kt × P

2 points. Clearer than 31. ...
K—B 1 (1 point); 32. B—K 4.

32. R × P

*

32. ...   Kt—B 5

1 point. 1 point also for 32. ...
K—K 2.

33. R—Kt 8 ch

*

33. ...   K—Q 2

1 point.

34. R × R

*

34. ...   K × R

1 point.

35. Q—Kt 8 ch

*

35. ...   K—Kt 2

1 point. Nothing for 35. ...
K—B 2; 36. Q—Q R 8. If now
36. B—K 4 ch, P—Q 4.

36. K—R 1

*

36. ...   Q—R 3

3 points. 37 Q × P ch, K—
Kt 3; leaves White with no
defence to his K R 2, so he is
forced to play . . .

37. Q—Kt 1

*

37. ...   Kt × B

2 points.

38. P × Kt

*

38. ...   R × P ch

3 points.

White resigns, for the pawn
ending which results is only a
formality.

Summary: In the long run, the
disadvantage of pawn weaknesses
is not so much the pawns themselves but the passive positioning
of the pieces which must result in
order to defend them. Here, Black
first reduced the scope of his
opponent's pieces on the queen's
side and was then able to obtain
a decisive attack on the other
wing.

Game No. 10

IN this game you have Black. Your consultation partner is Argentine grandmaster Hermann Pilnik. Your opponent is Hungarian grandmaster Laszlo Szabo. The game was played at Mar del Plata, Argentina, 1955. The first moves are 1. P—Q 4, Kt—K B 3; 2. P—Q B 4, P—K Kt 3; 3. Kt—Q B 3, B—Kt 2; 4. P—K 4, P—Q 3; 5. P—B 3, O—O; 6. B—K 3, Q Kt—Q 2; 7. Q—Q 2, P—B 4; 8. K Kt—K 2, R—K 1; 9. P × P, Q Kt × P; 10. Kt—Q 4, Kt—K 3; 11. B—K 2.

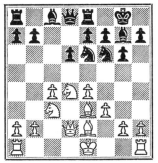

*
11. ...   Kt × Kt
2 points. 'Exchanges usually ease cramped positions.'
12. B × Kt
*
12. ...   B—K 3
1 point for this or the aggressive 12. ... Q—R 4.
13. O—O
*
13. ...   Q—R 4
1 point. Nothing for 13. ... R—Q B 1; when White can take

advantage of the undefended Q R P by 14. Kt—Q 5!, B × Kt; 15. K P × B, establishing a Q-side pawn majority and at the same time compelling Black to weaken his pawn formation by ... P—Q R 3 or ... P—Q Kt 3.
14. K R—Q 1
*
14. ...   Q R—B 1
2 points. Now if 15. Kt—Q 5, Q × Q; 16. R × Q, Kt × Kt (the Q R P can now be saved); 17. K P × Kt, B × B ch; 18. R × B, B—Q 2; 19. P—Q Kt 4 (to prevent the blockading 19. ... P—Q R 4), P—Kt 3; 20. P—Q R 4! and Black can draw the ending, since White is unable to keep his pawn majority mobile (the mobility is the decisive factor, not the majority itself). If 20. P—Q R 3 instead of 20. P—Q R 4, then 20. ... P—Q R 4; 21. R—Kt 1, R—R 1; 22. K—B 2, P × P; 23. P × P, R—R 7; and again Black has adequate counterplay.
15. P—Q Kt 3
*
15. ...   P—Q R 3
1 point. This is not strictly necessary, and Black could more logically aim for counterplay on the black squares by 15. ... Kt—Q 2 or 15. ... Kt—R 4 (2 points each).
16. Q—Kt 2
This decentralizing move loses much of the advantage which White has retained up to this point as a result of his 'Maroczy bind'

(pawns at Q B 4 and K 4 against pawn at Q 3) in the opening. 16. Q—K 3 was better.

*

16. ...   Kt—R 4
2 points. Clearly better than 16. ... Kt—Q 2; 17. B × B, K × B; 18. Kt—Q 5 dis. ch, followed by 19. P—Q Kt 4 (mobilizing the majority!) or than other moves, which allow 17 Kt—Q 5.
17. B × B

*

17. ...   Kt × B
1 point.
18. Q R—B 1

*

18. ...   R—B 2
2 points. Black intends ... K R —B 1 and ... P—Q Kt 4; he need no longer guard against 19. Kt— Q 5, since after 19. ... B × Kt; 20. K P × B (20. R × B is better, but harmless), Q—B 4 ch; followed by ... Kt—B 4; it is White who is in trouble. Other moves are also good here, e.g. 18. ... Kt—R 4; 18. ... Q—K 4; and 18. ... Q— K Kt 4 (all intending the black-square counterplay which is now suddenly available to Black after White's weak 16th move has weakened the two black diagonals converging at White's K 3). 1 point for each of these moves.
19. K—R 1

*

19. ...   Q—K 4
1 point for this or 19. ... K R— Q B 1.
20. Q—R 3 ?
Another weak decentralizing move. 20. Q—Q 2 was correct.

20. ...   Kt—R 4
1 point.
21. Kt—Q 5

*

21. ...   B × Kt
1 point.
22. R × B

*

22. ...   Q—B 5
2 points. More active than 22. ... Q—K 3, B 3, or Kt 2 (1 point each), 23. R(B 1)—Q 1.
23. R(B 1)—Q 1

*

23. ...   Q—R 3
3 points. This unusual move contains a nasty threat of 24. ... Kt—Kt 6 ch; followed by either ... Kt × B or ... Q—K 6 mate.
24. K—Kt 1
Forced.

*

24. ...   Q—K 6 ch
1 point.
25. K—B 1

*

25. ...   Kt—B 5
1 point.
26. R(Q 5)—Q 2

*

26. ...   R—B 4
3 points. Now Black has the deadly threat of 27. ... Kt—R 6!; 28. P × Kt, R—K Kt 4—note that all his last four moves have reiterated that the emphasis of his play is on the black squares.
27. Q—Kt 2

*

27. ...   Kt × P!
4 points, but deduct a point for 27. ... Kt—R 6; 28. Q—Q 4!
28. R—Q 5

If 28. K × Kt, R—Kt 4 ch;
29. K—R 3 (29. K—R 1, Q—B 7;
30. B—Q 3, Q × B P ch; 31. R—
Kt 2, Q × R(Q 8) ch) Q—B 7;
30. P—B 4, Q—Kt 7 ch; 31. K—
R 4, Q × P ch; 32. K × R, Q—
Kt 6 ch; 33. B—Kt 4, P—R 3 ch;
34. K × P, Q—R 5 ch; and mate
next move.

*

28. ...   R × R
1 point.
29. R × R

*

29. ...   P—K 3
3 points for this ingenious move,
which forces the win considerably
more quickly than 29. ... Kt—B 5
(2 points) or 29. ... Kt—R 5 (1
point).
30. R × P

*

30. ...   Q—B 5
1 point.
31. R—Q 7

*

31. ...   Q × R P
1 point.
32. Q—B 6

*

32. ...   R—K B 1
1 point.
33. P—B 5

*

33. ...   Kt—B 5
2 points. Neither 33. ... Q—
R 8 ch; 34. K—B 2, not 33. ... Kt
—K 6 ch; 34. K—K 1, lead to
anything clear-cut.
34. B—B 4

*

34. ...   Q—Kt 7 ch

1 point. Nothing for 34. ... Q—
R 6 ch; 35. K—B 2, Q—Kt 7 ch;
36. K—K 3, which makes the win
difficult.
35. K—K 1

*

35. ...   Q × B P
1 point.
36. Q—Q 4

*

36. ...   P—K R 4
3 points. Forwards! This pawn
can run straight through.
37. R × Kt P

*

37. ...   P—R 5
1 point.
38. Q—K 5

*

38. ...   R—Q 1
5 points for this sudden finish
(only 1 point for 38. ... P—R 6);
White resigns, for if 39. R—Kt 8
(else 39. ... R—Q 8 mate), Kt—
Kt 7 mate.

Summary: This game is an
object-lesson in the 'Maroczy
bind' position which arises when
White has pawns at Q B 4 and K 4
and Black a pawn at Q 3. White's
space advantage was achieved at
the cost of black-square weaknesses and it was his failure to
protect these sufficiently which was
the direct cause of his defeat. If
you had a bad score on this game,
look back and see whether this
was due to your underestimating
the extent to which Black's attack
operated against these black
square weaknesses.

Game No. 11

In this game you have Black. Your consultation partner is Carvalho, of Brazil. Your opponent is Primavera, of Italy. The game was played in the International Team Tournament at Helsinki, 1952.

The first moves are 1. P—Q 4, P—Q 4; 2. P—Q B 4, P—K 3; 3. Kt—Q B 3, P—Q B 4; 4. B P × P, K P × P; 5. Kt—B 3, Kt—Q B 3; 6. P—K Kt 3, P—B 5; 7. B—Kt 2, B—Q Kt 5; 8. O—O, K Kt—K 2; 9. B—B 4, O—O; 10. Kt—K 1.

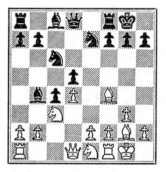

*

10. ...   B—Kt 5

3 points. The outstanding characteristic of this position is Black's mobile majority of pawns on the queen's side. The player with a queen's side majority should almost always aim at transposing into an end-game, where a majority of wing pawns can result in a passed pawn with the enemy king still on the other side of the board. However, as compensation for Black's queen's side majority, White has a majority in the centre, and if he can force the advance P—K 4, Black's Q B P will become isolated and an easy object of attack. Black could prevent P—K 4 directly by 10. ... P—B 4 (1 point); but his Q P would then be subject to attack by White's minor pieces, e.g. 11. Kt—B 2, B—R 4; 12. Kt—K 3, B—K 3; 13. B—Kt 5. Black therefore holds back P—K 4 by indirect means, based on the fact that if White advances without due preparation, his Q P will become very weak.

11. Kt—B 2

*

11. ...   B—Q R 4

1 point. Deduct a point for 11. ... B—Q 3; 12. Kt × P, Kt × Kt; 13. B × Kt, B × B; 14. B × Kt.

12. P—K R 3

*

12. ...   B—K 3

2 points. 12. ... B—B 4 (1 point) seems more elastic, but, then comes 13. P—K 4!, B × Kt (13. ... P × P; 14. Kt—K 3); 14. Kt P × B, B × K P; 15. B × B, P × B; 16. Q—K 2, regaining the pawn with an excellent game for White.

13. K—R 2

(13. P—K 4 was better, although after 13. ... P—B 4 !; Black keeps the position blocked.)

*
13. ...   Q—Q 2

2 points. This not only prepares to complete his development, but, by strengthening his position on the Q file, acts as a further deterrent to P—K 4. 1 point for the direct ... P—B 4; when a later B—K Kt 5 × Kt would still ease White's position somewhat.

14. P—B 3

*
14. ...   Q R—Q 1

2 points. 1 point for 14. ... P—B 4.

15. Q—Q 2

*
15. ...   Kt—Kt 3

2 points. This is to permit ... P—B 4; without a resulting pin of the K Kt.

16. B—Kt 5

*
16. ...   P—B 3

1 point. This is, of course, the only consistent continuation.

17. B—K 3

*
17. ...   P—B 4

1 point.

18. B—Kt 5

*
18. ...   Q R—K 1

2 points. Here the rook continues to discourage any advance of White's K P; but 18. ... R—Kt 1 (2 points), intending ... P—Q Kt 4 as quickly as possible, is also playable. Deduct 2 points for the self-pins 18. ... Q Kt—K 2? and 18. ... K Kt—K 2?

19. P—K 3

*
19. ...   P—Kt 4

1 point. Owing to the pin, the mobilizing of his pawn majority requires no further preparation.

20. P—R 3

*
20. ...   P—Q R 3

1 point. An advantage of ... Q R—Kt 1 two moves ago would have been that this preparation for a further advance of the Q Kt P would not now be necessary; instead he could have played 20. ... B—Q B 2; followed by P—Q R 4.

21. Q R—K 1

*
21. ...   P—R 3

1 point (and 1 point if you chose it last move). Black acquires the two bishops before proceeding further.

22. B—B 4

*
22. ...   Kt × B

1 point.

23. K P × Kt?

This helps Black a lot. 23. Kt P × Kt was much better.

*
23. ...   B—K B 2

3 points. A distant pawn majority almost always becomes more important as pieces are exchanged and the ending approaches. So Black forces the

33

exchange of all the heavy pieces on the only open file, which White can scarcely avoid, as otherwise Black could double or triple his queen and rooks on the K file and eventually penetrate into his opponent's position. 23. ... B—Kt 3 (2 points), tying White down to the defence of the Q P, is also strong here. Deduct a point for 23. ... P—Kt 5?; since it is most important for Black to keep his pawns united in order to facilitate the eventual creation of a passed pawn.

24. R × R

*

24. ...   R × R

1 point.

25. R—K 1

*

25. ...   R × R

1 point for this, 25. ... R—K 2; or 25. ... R—K 3.

26. Q × R

*

26. ...   Q—K 3

1 point.

27. Q × Q

*

27. ...   B × Q

1 point.

28. K—Kt 1

*

28. ...   B—Kt 3

2 points. The weakness of the Q P facilitates the further advance of Black's pawn majority, and underlines White's mistake in capturing with the K P on move 23.

29. Kt—K 2

*

29. ...   P—Q R 4

1 point.

30. K—B 2

*

30. ...   P—Kt 5

1 point.

31. P × P

*

31. ...   P × P

1 point.

32. K—K 3

*

32. ...   K—B 2

1 point.

33. P—Kt 4

*

33. ...   P—Kt 3

1 point. Naturally Black does not obligingly undouble the pawns by 33. ... P × P? (deduct 3 points).

34. P—R 4

*

34. ...   P—R 4

3 points. This finally fixes the pawns, and prevents White's last hope of a swindle by B—R 3 and P—R 5.

35. P—Kt 5

*

35. ...   B—B 1!

3 points. To bring the remaining minor piece into play is much more convincing than 35. ... B—R 4 (1 point); or 35. ... P—Kt 6

(deduct 1 point, since after 36. Kt —R 3!, B—R 4; 37. Kt—Q Kt 1, Black has no easy job to break through).

36. B—B 1

*

36. ...   B—R 3

1 point.

37. K—Q 2

*

37. ...   K—K 3

1 point.

38. K—K 3

*

38. ...   B—Kt 4

1 point, and 1 point if you chose this last move.

39. B—R 3

*

39. ...   B—R 5

1 point.

40. Kt—R 1

*

40. ...   B—Q 8

2 points. A pawn must fall.

41. B—Kt 2

*

41. ...   B × Kt

1 point.

42. K × B

*

42. ...   P—Kt 6

2 points. Even stronger than capturing the pawn at once (1 point).

43. K—Q 2

*

43. ...   B × P

1 point.

White resigns.

Summary: Basically, the lesson to be drawn from this game is simple. When you have a queen's side pawn majority, assuming that it is mobile and not under attack from your opponent's pieces, you can play for the ending and exchange pieces with confidence. If you failed to obtain a good score on this game, it means that you have not been fully aware of this rule.

Game No. 12

IN this game you have White. Your consultation partner is David Bronstein, world championship candidate and one of the most likeable and friendly of all the grandmasters. Your opponent is former British champion Harry Golombek. The game was played in the Alekhine Memorial tournament, Moscow, 1956.

The first moves are 1. P—Q 4, Kt—K B 3; 2. P—Q B 4, P—K 3; 3. Kt—Q B 3, B—Kt 5; 4. Kt—B 3, P—Q Kt 3; 5. P—K 3, B—Kt 2; 6. B—Q 3, Kt—K 5; 7. O—O, B × Kt; 8. P × B, O—O; 9. Kt—K 1, P—K B 4; 10. P—B 3, Kt—K B 3; 11. P—Q R 4, Kt—B 3.

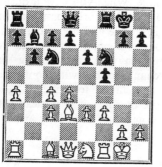

*

12. P—K 4

2 points. The type of position in the diagram frequently results from the Nimzo-Indian Defence, and is critical for both sides. Both players must hasten forward with their respective plans. White's theme is the opening of the centre for his two bishops and, eventually, a king's side attack. Black must try to tie his opponent down to the defence of his front Q B P by such moves as ... Kt—Q R 4; ... B—R 3; ... P—B 4; and ... R—B 1. Hence, there is no credit for passive moves like 12. Kt—B 2. 1 point for 12. Q—B 2, 12. Q—K 2, or 12. B—R 3.

12. ...   P × P

*

13. P × P

1 point.

13. ...   P—K 4

*

14. B—Kt 5

3 points.

14. P—Q 5 (1 point), Kt—Q R 4; would block the position (to the disadvantage of White's bishops) and also drive the black Q Kt where it wants to go, while 14. P × P (no credit) would give Black's knights too much scope. 14. Kt—B 3 and 14. B—K 3 (2 points each) are quite playable but less aggressive than the text.

14. ...   Q—K 2

Not 14. ... P × P; 15. P × P, Kt × Q P?; 16. P—K 5.

*

15. Kt—B 2

1 point.

Safeguarding the attacked Q P.

15. ...   Q —Q 3

*

16. B—R 4

4 points. Black was now threatening to win the Q P, but this fine move prevents it. If now 16. ... P × P; 17. B—Kt 3, Q—B 4;

18. P × P, Kt × Q P?; 19. B—
B 2. 1 point only for 16. P—Q 5
and no credit for 16. P × P.

16. ...   QR—K 1

*

17. B—Kt 3

2 points. Again clearly best; the
pin on the K P forces Black to
retract his 15th move.

17. ...   Q—K 2

*

18. Kt—K 3

3 points. Once again White
avoids the fixing of his central
pawns by neat tactics: 18. ... P ×
P; 19. Kt—B 5. Still no credit for
18. P—Q 5 or 18. P × P.

18. ...   P—Q 3

*

19. B—R 4

4 points. The shuttling to and
fro of the bishop seems curious,
but is quite logical in the light of
White's plans to obtain the pair of
bishops. 2 points for 19. Kt—B 5,
19. Kt—Q 5, and 19. R—R 2
(preparing to double rooks) which
are all reasonable moves without
having the same force as the text.

19. ...   Kt—Q 1

*

20. Kt—Q 5
1 point.

20. ...   B × Kt

*

21. B P × B

2 points. This is much better
than 21. K P × B (no credit);
White threatens 22. B—Q Kt 5.
Having obtained the pair of

bishops, White's next problem is
to open up the game so that they
will be fully effective.

21. ...   P—B 3

*

22. Q—Kt 3

3 points. 22. P × B P (2 points)
is good and logical, but White can
take his time and strengthen the
position still further before making
the move, since 22. ... B P × P;
still fails to 23. B—Q Kt 5.

22. ...   K—R 1

*

23. Q R—K 1

2 points. 1 point for 23. P ×
B P, 23. R—B 2, or 23. R—R 2.

23. ...   P—K R 3

*

24. Q—R 3

5 points. Perhaps the most
difficult move of the game, which
sets up a concealed threat to the
black queen which prevents Black
easing his game by ... P—K Kt 4
and ... Kt—R 4, e.g. 24. ... P—
K Kt 4; 25. B—Kt 3, Kt—R 4;
26. P × K P, P × K P (26. ...
Kt × B; 27. P × Q P); 27. B ×
P ch. The immediate 24. B—Kt 3
(1 point) does not transpose
because of 24. ... Kt—R 4. 2
points, again, for 24. P × B P.
It is worth noting that 24. P ×
K P, Q P × P; 25. P—B 4, P—
B 4; although it secures a sup-
ported passed pawn for White,
would ease Black's game considerably since the pawn can be
blockaded by a black knight
at Q 3.

24. ...   P—K Kt 4

37

*
25. B—Kt 3
1 point.
25. ...   Kt—Q 2

*
26. P × B P
2 points. At last this move is necessary, since Black could otherwise play 26. ... B P × P.
26. ...   Kt × P

*
27. B—Kt 5
2 points.
27. ...   R × R ch

*
28. R × R
1 point.
28. ...   Kt(B 3)—Kt 1

*
29. B—Q B 4
2 points. White threatens 30. R—B 7, and his bishops now begin to come into their own.
29. ...   R—K B 1

*
30. R × R ch
1 point.
30. ...   Q × R

*
31. P × P
1 point. This wins a pawn, since 31. ... Kt × P; loses a piece.
31. ...   Kt—B 4

*
32. P × P
1 point.
32. ...   Kt × K P

*
33. P—Q 7
3 points. 3 points for 33. B—K 5 ch, which also wins speedily.
33. ...   Kt—B 4
If 33. ... Q × Q; 34. P—Q 8 (Q) ch wins.

*
34. B—K 5 ch
1 point.
34. ...   K—R 2

*
35. B—Q 3 ch
2 points. Black resigns, for if 35. ... K—Kt 1; 36. Q—R 2 ch.

Summary: This game illustrates how strategical ends (in this case the acquiring of the two bishops and the opening of the position in their favour) can be achieved by tactical means. This type of situation is one of the most difficult for the amateur player to handle, since it involves simultaneously making general judgments and working out particular variations.

Game No. 13

IN this game you have Black. Your consultation partner is Samuel Reshevsky, the best player in the world outside Russia. Your opponent is Abe Turner. The game was played in the Rosenwald tournament in New York in 1956. The first moves are 1. P—Q 4, Kt—K B 3; 2. P—Q B 4, P—K 3; 3. Kt—Q B 3, B—Kt 5; 4. Q—B 2, P—B 4; 5. P × P, O—O; 6. B—B 4, B × P; 7. P—K 3, Kt—R 4; 8. B—Kt 3, Kt—Q B 3; 9. B—K 2, Kt × B; 10. R P × Kt.

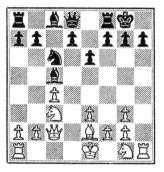

*
10. ...   P—K R 3

2 points. It is always a problem how to defend against a mate threatened in this way. In this case 10. ... P—K Kt 3 would place too many of Black's pawns on white squares, thus handicapping his Q B, and would not eliminate the danger of White's queen eventually penetrating to K R 6. 10 ... P—B 4; would be an outright mistake here because of the reply 11. P—K Kt 4, dissolving the doubled pawns and opening the king's side still further.

11. R—Q 1
*
11. ...   P—Q Kt 3

2 points. Black does not need to bother greatly about his opponent's open K R file for the time being, since White's minor pieces cannot easily join in the attack. This move is a more active method of developing the Q B than ... P—Q 3 and ... B—Q 2.

12. Kt—B 3
*
12. ...   B—Kt 2
1 point.

13. P—K Kt 4
*
13. ...   B—K 2

1 point. Now P—Kt 5 was a threat, and Black wished to avoid a further loosening of his pawn formation.

14. Q—Kt 1
*
14. ...   R—B 1

2 points. Black pursues the well-known strategy, common to many of the Indian defences, of bringing about weaknesses in the enemy pawn formation by the action of his pieces before committing his own pawns to a particular formation. 14. ... P—Q 3 (1 point); is playable, but if 14. ... Q—B 2; 15. Kt—Q Kt 5, and if the Q retires to Q Kt 1, the Q R is blocked,

39

while otherwise White can post his knight on the strong outpost Q 6.

15. O—O

Admitting that his attack has no future.

*

15. ...   P—Q 3

1 point. 15. ... Q—B 2 (1 point) is also playable now; if 16. Kt—Q Kt 5, Q—Kt 1.

16. R—B 1

*

16. ...   Q—B 2

1 point for this; but 2 points for Q—Q 2, which avoids White's next move.

17. Kt—Q 5

*

17. ...   Q—Q 2

2 points. Nothing for 17. ... P × Kt; 18. P × P when, after White recovers his piece, his K B 5 will eventually become available as an outpost for his knight.

18. Kt—B 3

Inconsistent. White should follow up his last move with 18. Kt × B ch, with equality; but White has hopes that his opponent will now tamely acquiesce in a draw by repetition of moves with 18. ... Q—B 2; 19. Kt—Q 5, etc.

*

18. ...   K R—Q 1

2 points for this or 18. ... B—B 3.

19. K R—Q 1

*

19. ...   B—B 3

1 point.

20. Kt—K 4

*

20. ...   Q—K 2

2 points. Now if 21. Kt × B ch, Q × Kt; Black's queen is aggressively posted. If, on the other hand 20. ... B—K 2; White gains some advantage by 21. P—B 5.

21. Kt—B 3

*

21. ...   Kt—R 4

2 points. Having completed his development, Black now begins the systematic weakening of his opponent's pawn formation.

22. Kt—Q Kt 5

*

22. ...   P—R 3

1 point. If 23. Kt—R 7?, R—R 1.

23. Q Kt —Q 4

*

23. ...   P—Kt 3

1 point. With a sound position, Black awaits further developments. This move is no longer weakening, since White has long since abandoned any pretensions to a king's side attack. Also good are 23. ... R—B 2 and 23. ... Kt—B 3 (1 point each).

24. P—Kt 4

*

24. ...   Kt—B 3

1 point.

25. P—R 3

*

25. ...   K—Kt 2

1 point for this, Kt × Kt or R—B 2.

26. B—Q 3

*

26. ...   Kt × Kt

1 point for this or R—B 2.

27. Kt × Kt

*

27. ...   R—B 2

1 point.

28. B—K 2

*

28. ...   K R—Q B 1

1 point. Although Black cannot expect to win the Q B P for some time to come, the pressure on it ties up White's pieces.

29. Kt—Kt 3

*

29. ...   B—K 4

3 points. This is made with the object of inducing a further weakening of the pawns; if 30. P—B 4, B—K B 3; Black will aim eventually at establishing his K B or queen on K Kt 6. However, this was better than the line White actually chooses.

30. Kt—Q 2

*

30. ...   Q—B 3

3 points. Now ... B—Kt 7 is constantly in the air.

31. Kt—B 1

*

31. ...   B—B 3

3 points. Black intends ... B—R 5; or if 32. P—Q Kt 5, P × P; 33. P × P, B—Q 4; and in either case the bishops, working in their ideal situation of parallel or criss-cross diagonals, become very active.

32. R—K 1

*

32. ...   B—R 5

1 point.

33. B—Q 1

A blunder; 33. Q—R 2 offered a longer resistance.

*

33. ...   B × B

1 point.

34. R(B 1) × B

*

34. ...   R × P

1 point.

35. P—B 3

*

35. ...   P—Q 4

1 point for this or for 35. ... R—B 7.

36. R—Q 3

*

36. ...   R—B 7

1 point.

37. R(K 1)—Q 1

*

37. ...   R—Kt 7

2 points. White's queen is now lost.

38. Q—R 1

41

*

38. ...   R × P ch
1 point.
39. K × R

*

39. ...   B × Q
1 point.
40. Kt—Kt 3

*

40. ...   R—B 7 ch
1 point for this, Q—Kt 7 ch,
or R—B 6.

41. R(1)—Q 2

*

41. ...   Q—Kt 7
1 point for this or R × R ch.

42. Kt—B 1

*

42. ...   R × R ch
1 point.
43. R × R

*

43. ...   Q × R P
1 point.

White resigns.

Summary: This game particularly shows the technique to be
adopted when the opponent makes
no effort to seize the initiative but
waits for you to 'come and get
him'. In these circumstances you
have time to regroup your pieces
on to their most aggressive and
mutually supporting squares before undertaking an all-out attack.
Note particularly the quiet way in
which Reshevsky strengthens his
position slightly but definitely on
moves 23, 25, 29, 30, and 31—
these moves are of the essence of
great positional play.

Game No. 14

IN this game you have White. Your consultation partner is Boris Spassky, World Junior Champion and already recognized as a great master. Your opponent is Paul Keres. The game was played in the U.S.S.R. Championship, 1957. The first moves are 1. P—Q 4, Kt—K B 3; 2. P—Q B 4, P—K 3; 3. Kt—Q B 3, B—Kt 5; 4. B— Kt 5, P—K R 3; 5. B—R 4, P— B 4; 6. P—Q 5, P—Q 3; 7. P— K 3, P—K 4; 8. Q—B 2, Q Kt— Q 2.

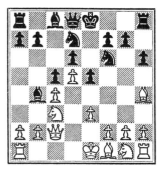

*
9. Kt—K 2

2 points. In this opening the position tends to be blocked and favours knights rather than bishops; consequently Black aims at keeping the game closed, while White, having forced the exchange of his opponent's K B, will try to open up diagonals so that his pair of bishops begin to count. Naturally he wishes to avoid doubled pawns in the process, and since 9. P—Q R 3 (no credit) would be a mistake because of 9. ... B ×

Kt ch; 10. Q × B?, Kt × P!; the text move is logical.

9. ...   Kt—B 1

*
10. P—Q R 3
1 point.
10. ...   B × Kt ch.

*
11. Kt × B
1 point.
11. ...   Kt—Kt 3

*
12. B—Kt 3
1 point. 12. B × Kt? would, of course, be quite inconsistent.

12. ...   Kt—R 4

*
13. B—Q 3
1 point. This ensures that if Black now exchanges one of the bishops, he will have some positional difficulties after 13. ... Kt × B; 14. R P × Kt, Kt—K 2 (14. ... Q—B 3; 15. Kt—Kt 5); 15. P—B 4, P—B 3; 16. B—Kt 6 ch. Nothing for other moves, which allow Black to play ... Kt × B in complete safety.

13. ...   Kt—K 2

*
14. P—B 4
1 point. White is still ready to transpose into the variation given in the last note. 14. B—R 4 would be a mistake because of 14. ... P— K Kt 4; 15. B—Kt 3, P—B 4; threatening ... P—B 5.

14. ...   P × P

*
15. P × P

1 point. It is difficult to say whether the doubled K Kt Ps which result from this are more or less weak than those which arise after 15. B × P (1 point), P—K Kt 4; 16. B—Kt 3, Kt × B.

15. ...   P—B 4

This pawn becomes a target for attack as well as restricting the scope of Black's bishop; 15. ... O—O; is preferable.

*
16. O—O

2 points. 16. O—O—O (1 point) is rather too risky here; Black is well placed to begin a quick counter-attack by ... P—Q R 3 and ... P—Q Kt 4.

16. ...   Kt × B

*
17. P × Kt

1 point.

17. ...   O—O

*
18. Q R—K 1

1 point for this or 18. K R—K 1, and 1 point for 18. Kt—Q 1, aiming to put pressure on the weak K B P by Kt—K 3.

18. ...   B—Q 2

*
19. R—K 2

1 point for this, 19. Kt—Q 1 or 19. R—B 2.

19. ...   K—R 1

*
20. R (B 1)—K 1

1 point.

20. ...   Kt—Kt 1

*
21. Kt—Q 1

1 point.

21. ...   Q—B 3

*
22. Q—B 3

4 points. An instructive decision —positional weaknesses like vulnerable pawns and 'bad' bishops are best exploited in the ending, since as pieces become exchanged, the weaknesses become more apparent and easier to attack. Here 22. Kt —K 3 (1 point), Q R—K 1; makes it difficult for White to make progress, since Q—B 3 would now result in White himself having his pawn formation dislocated.

22. ...   P—R 3

Better 22. ... Q—B 2; although after 23. Kt—K 3, the natural 23. ... Q R—K 1 leads to a further loosening of the pawns by 24. Q—R 5.

*
23. Q × Q

1 point.

23. ...   Kt × Q

*
24. Kt—K 3

1 point.

24. ...   Kt—Kt 1

44

*
25. P—Q Kt 4

2 points. Another example of the 'alternation' strategy characteristic of much present-day master play. Having pinned Black down to the defence of a weakness on one wing, White now transfers his attention to the other. The preparatory move 25. R—Kt 1 (1 point) is not so good since after 25. ... P—Q R 4; 26. P—Q Kt 4, R P × P; Black has the open Q R file for counter-attack. A noncommittal move like 25. K—B 2 (1 point) would also allow Black to defend his queen's wing in the same way.

25. ...   Q R—B 1

*
26. R—Kt 1

1 point. White threatens P × P, which is also good at once (1 point).

26. ...   P—Q Kt 4

Strategically outplayed, Black tries to 'mix it' tactically.

*
27. B P × P

1 point for this or 27. Kt P × P.

27. ...   R P × P

*
28. P × P

1 point. Now Black is left with a second weak pawn on Q Kt 4.

28. ...   R × P

*
29. R(K 2)—Kt 2

2 points. Not only good, but necessary, since Black threatened

to simplify into a drawn position by 29. ... R—B 6, which would now be answered by 30. R—Kt 3.

29. ...   R—K 1

*
30. B × B P

3 points. 30. K—B 2 (1 point) would also win in time, but 30. Kt × P (deduct 2 points) is a blunder because of 30. ... R × P. If now 30. ... B × B; 31. Kt × B, R × P; 32. R × P, R × R; 33. R × R, and White's Q R P decides the issue.

30. ...   R × Kt

*
31. B × B

1 point.

31. ...   R × Kt P

*
32. R × P

1 point. If 32. ... R × R; 33. R × R, R × P; 34. R—Kt 8, K—R 2; 35. B—B 5 ch, P—Kt 3; 36. B × P ch, K × B; 37. R × Kt ch, K—B 2; 38. R—Q 8, K—K 2; 39. R—K R 8, R—Q 6; 40. R × P, R × P; and the ending of rook and two united pawns against rook and pawn is won for White.

32. ...   R—B 7

*
33. B—R 3

2 points.

33. ...   R × R P

*
34. R—Kt 8

1 point.

34. ...   R × B

Despair, but if 34. ... R(R 6)—R 7; 35. R—Q 8 is sufficient.

*
35. P × R
1 point.
35. ...   R—Q 7

*
36. R—Q 8
1 point. The most decisive, because most aggressive. White again threatens to win the knight.
36. ...   K—R 2

*
37. R × P
1 point.
37. ...   Kt—K 2

*
38. R—Q 7
3 points for this. The point of Black's exchange sacrifice was that this ending can easily be drawn if White permits himself a moment of carelessness, e.g. 38. R—Kt 7?, R × P!; 39. R × R, Kt × R: with a draw. White can also win by 38. R—Kt 5 (2 points), but the text is prettier. The idea is that if 38. ... Kt × P; 39. P—B 5! (but not 39. R—Kt 5, R—Q 8 ch; 40. K—B 2, Kt—K 6; or 39. R(1)—Kt 7, K—Kt 3; 40. R × P ch, K—B 4; and in either case Black has good chances of saving the game), Kt—B 6; 40. R × R, Kt × R; 41. R—Q 3!, when Black's knight is without a move and can be simply captured by White's king.
38. ...   Kt—B 4

*
39. R—Kt 6
2 points. Again much the most exact move, since it prevents Black

obtaining counterplay by ... K—Kt 3—R 4—R 5.
39. ...   Kt—K 6

*
40. P—Q 6
2 points.
40. ...   Kt—B 4

*
41. K—B 1
1 point. 1 point also for 41. R—Q 8.
41. ...   Kt—Q 5

*
42. R—R 7
1 point for this, 42. R—K 7, 42. R—Q 8, 42. R—Q B 7, or 42. (R Q 7)—Kt 7.
42. ...   Kt—K3

*
43. P—B 5
1 point.
43. ...   Kt—B 4

*
44. P—B 6
1 point.
Black resigns.

Summary: White's win here is a triumph of logic; once Black creates a positional weakness, his pieces are first tied down to its defence, and then White makes a winning break-through on the opposite wing. Conversely, if you had a poor score on this game it indicates that you tend to make moves which are irrelevant to the main theme of your strategy; you can avoid this by testing each move before you actually make it, according to its relation to your plan.

IV ATTACKING PLAY

Game No. 15

IN this game you have White. Your consultation partner is former world champion Dr. Max Euwe. Your opponent is the Italian master V. Nestler. The game was played in the Lenzerheide (Switzerland) team tournament, 1956.

The first moves are 1. P—Q 4, Kt—K B 3; 2. P—Q B 4, P—Q 3; 3. P—K Kt 3, Q Kt—Q 2; 4. B—Kt 2, P—K 4; 5. Kt—K B 3, P—B 3; 6. O—O, B—K 2; 7. Kt—B 3, O—O; 8. Q—B 2, Q—B 2; 9. P—Kt 3, R—K 1; 10. B—Kt 2, Kt—B 1.

*

11. P—B 5

5 points. This surprising advance leads in a few moves to a clarification of the central position in White's favour. Quieter moves which are reasonable here are 11. P—K 4, 11. K R—Q 1, and

11. Q R—Q 1 (2 points each).

Nothing, however, for 11 P × P; experience has taught that the straightforward central exchange in such positions, which usually arise from the King's Indian and Old Indian Defences, leads to speedy equality.

11. ...   Kt—Kt 3

If 11. ... Q P × P; 12. P × K P, Kt(B 3)—Q 2; 13. Kt—K 4, Kt—K Kt 3; 14. Q—B 3, B—B 1; 15. Kt—Q 6!, while if 11. ... K P × P; Dr. Euwe had prepared 12. P × P, Q × P; 13. Q R—Q 1, P—B 4; 14. P—K 3, regaining the pawn advantageously.

*

12. P × QP

1 point.

12. ...   B × P

*

13. Q R—B 1

2 points. Much the strongest, since it threatens to obtain the two bishops and simultaneously open the game by the neat combination 14. Kt—Q Kt 5!—an idea well worth remembering.

13. ...   Q—K 2

*

14. P × P

1 point. Otherwise Black has serious counterplay by 14. ... P—K 5.

14. ...   Kt × P

47

*
15. Kt × Kt

1 point.

15. ...   B × Kt

*
16. P—K 4

3 points. Black cannot now win a pawn by 16. ... B × Kt; 17. Q × B, because of the mate threat. The interest of this position lies in the values of the respective pawn majorities. Black has 3 to 2 on the queen's side, and experience teaches us that, other things being equal, the player with the queen's side majority has the better game. Two factors outweigh this judgment in the present position. Firstly, it is exceptionally difficult for Black to mobilize his majority owing to White's command of the half-open Q B file and the long white diagonal. Secondly, White's own majority is a serious threat since P—K B 4 and P—K 5 can follow with gain of tempo, while the majority is backed by a well-situated bishop on Q Kt 2. Dr. Euwe considers, in fact, that this position is strategically won for White.

16. ...   B—Q 2

*
17. P—K R 3

2 points. Deduct 2 points for the over-hasty 17. P—B 4, B—Q 5 ch; 18. K—R 1, Kt—Kt 5.

17. ...   P—K R 3

*
18. P—B 4

1 point.

18. ...   B—Q 5 ch

*
19. K—R 2

2 points; slightly better than 19. K—R 1 (1 point) because it gives an extra guard to the K Kt P and K R P.

19. ...   B—Kt 3

*
20. P—K 5

1 point.

20. ...   Kt—R 2

*
21. Q R—K 1

2 points. This is the natural way of preparing for a further advance of the pawn majority by P—B 5. 21. Q R—Q 1 (1 point) is less forcing.

21. ...   B—R 4

*
22. P—B 5

1 point.

22. ...   B—B 2

*
23. Kt—R 4

3 points. 23. P—B 6 (1 point), P × P; 24. P × P, Q—Q 3 would allow Black some counterplay, as his bishops are rather dangerously directed towards White's king. However, White does not need to hurry with P—B 6 (Black can never prevent it by ... P—B 3; because of P—K 6), and so first regroups his pieces on to better squares. 23. Kt—Kt 5 and 23. Kt—Q 5 (1 point each) are playable, but White's advantage is much reduced after 23. ... P × Kt; 24. Q × B, B—B 3.

23. ...   Q R—Q 1

*

24. Kt—B 5

2 points.

24. ...   B—B 1

*

25. Kt—Q 3

1 point. Now the knight is ready to join in the action against the king's side.

25. ...   Q—Q 2

*

26. R—Q 1

2 points. Not 26. B—K 4 (no credit), Kt—Kt 4; but now White threatens 27. Kt—B 4, Q × P?; 28. B—K 4.

26. ...   Q—K 2

*

27. P—K R 4

2 points. White still doesn't hurry with P—B 6 (1 point); first he takes away all the possible sting from Black's counterplay once the position is opened. This move deprives Black's knight of K Kt 4.

27. ...   P—K Kt 3

This hastens the end, but otherwise White would continue 28. Q—B 1, strengthening P—B 6 owing to the queen's aiming at the K R P.

*

28. P × P

2 points. Not 28. P—K 6 (deduct 2 points), Q × P ch!

28. ...   P × P

*

29. Kt—B 4

2 points.

29. ...   B—B 4

*

30. Q—B 4 ch

2 points. This wins a pawn, for if 30. ... Q—B 2; 31. P—K 6, B × P; 32. Q—B 3, and wins, or if 30. ... K—Kt 2; 31. P—K 6 dis. ch, Kt—B 3; 32. Kt—R 5 ch!, P × Kt; 33. R × B!, R—K B 1; 34. R(Q 1)—K B 1. Or 30. ... K—Kt 2; 31. P—K 6 dis. ch., K—Kt 1; 32. R—Q 7!, R × R; 33. P × R dis. ch.

30. ...   B—K 3

*

31. Kt × P

4 points. Now if 31. ... B × Q; 32. Kt × Q ch, R × Kt; 33. R × R ch, B × R; 34. P × B, and White wins the ending.

31. ...   Q—Kt 2

*

32. R × R

4 points. 3 points for 32. Q—B 2. The text contains another trap, for if 32. ... B × Q; 33. R × R ch, etc.

32. ...   B × R

*

33. Q—B 2

1 point.

33. ...   B—Q B 2

*

34. Kt—B 4

49

2 points. Now the threats include Kt × B and Kt—R 5.

34. ...   B × K P

*

35. B × B

1 point.

Black resigns.

His last move was a blunder, costing at least a rook after 35. ... Q × B; 36. Q—Kt 6 ch.

Summary: The great lesson to be learnt from this game is that an attack must be nursed carefully if the opponent has pieces, like Black's two bishops in this game, which may benefit from the sudden opening of the position. If you chose a more obvious and forcing move at White's 17th, 23rd, 24th, 27th, or 28th, it probably means you tend to rush your attacks and do not pay sufficient indication to the preliminary preparation. If you went wrong on White's 30th, 31st, or 32nd moves, then you should make a greater effort to calculate all the consequences if there are tactical opportunities and forced series of moves present in the position.

Game No. 16

IN this game you have Black. Your consultation partner is G. Durasevic, rising young Yugoslav star. Your opponent is Victor Korchnoi, joint winner of the Hastings 1955-6 tournament. The game was played in the U.S.S.R. *v.* Yugoslavia match, Belgrade, 1956.

The first moves are 1. P—Q 4, Kt—K B 3; 2. P—Q B 4, P—K 3; 3. Kt—Q B 3, B—Kt 5; 4. B—Kt 5, P—B 4; 5. P—Q 5, P—K R 3; 6. B—R 4, P—Q Kt 4; 7. P—K 4, P—Q 3; 8. Q—B 2, O—O; 9. Q P × P, Kt—Q B 3; 10. Kt—B 3, B × P; 11. P × P.

*

11. ...   Kt—Q 5

2 points for this typical gambit play. Black's pawn sacrifice on move 6 was based on White's exposed K and pinned Q Kt, plus Black's considerable advantage in development.

12. Kt × Kt

*

12. ...   P × Kt

1 point.

13. P—Q R 3

*

13. ...   B—R 4

4 points. 13. ... Q—R 4 (1 point) looks still better, but after 14. B × Kt (exchanging a black minor piece which is very useful as the game goes), P × B; 15. R—B 1, P × Kt; 16. P × B, Black's attack has suddenly disappeared.

14. P—Q Kt 4

*

14. ...   P—Kt 4

5 points. With a pawn down, Black must make every move count. If 14. ... B × P (2 points), White just escapes by 15. P × B, P × Kt; 16. Q × P, R—B 1; 17. B × Kt!, P × B; 18. Q—Kt 3 ch, K—R 1; 19. B—K 2. If 14. ... P × Kt (3 points); 15. P × B, Q × P; 16. B × Kt, P × B; 17. B—Q 3, and, although the passed Q B P is powerful, White still has counter-chances owing to the break-up of Black's king's side.

15. B—Kt 3

*

15. ...   R—B 1

5 points. 6 points if you chose this on the last move, where it was equally playable. Other alternatives are not so clear, e.g. 15. ... P × Kt (2 points); 16. P × B, Q × P; 17. B × P (with B—Kt 4 as a resource), or 15. ... B × P (1 point); 16. P × B, P × Kt; 17. Q × P, Kt × P; 18. Q—Q 4.

16. P × B

51

*

16. ...   R × Kt

2 points.

17. Q—Q 2

*

17. ...   Kt × P

2 points.

18. Q × P

*

18. ...   Q × P

4 points. If now 19. Q × Kt,
R—B 8 db. ch.

19. Q—Kt 4

*

19. ...   Q × Q

2 points.

20. P × Q

*

20. ...   R—K 1

5 points. The concealed threat
on the K file now makes it impossible for White to complete his
development, e.g. 21. B—K 2,
B—B 5!; 22. B × B, Kt × B dis.
ch; 23. K—Q 2, Kt—K 5 ch;
followed by ... R × B.

21. P—B 3

*

21. ...   R—K 6 ch

4 points. Nothing for the un-
clear 21. ... Kt × B; 22. P × Kt,
B—B 5 dis. ch.; 23. K—B 2.

22. K—Q 1

*

22. ...   B—Kt 6 ch

3 points.

23. K—B 1

*

23. ...   R—B 1 ch

3 points.

24. K—Kt 2

*

24. ...   R—B 7 ch

2 points.

25. K—R 3

*

25. ...   R—Q 7

6 points. This quiet move forces
White's immediate resignation.

Summary: This game demon-
strates very clearly the need to
make every move count when a
sacrificial attack is in progress. If
you went wrong on moves 13, 14,
or 15, it shows that you need to be
more careful and thorough when
working out the possible variations in a position. Another
principle exemplified in this game
is that an attack can still be
successful when the queens are
exchanged, always provided that
the remaining attacking pieces can
be well co-ordinated. Finally,
White's difficulties arose from his
failure to castle in the early opening; if a king is in the centre and
the central files can be opened, all
sorts of sacrificial combinations
become possible (compare with
game No. 27).

Game No. 17

In this game you have White. Your consultation partner is the veteran Czech player J. Rejfír. Your opponent is the Austrian international Josef Lokvenc. The game was played in the match Czechoslovakia *v.* Austria, 1956. The first moves are 1. P—Q B 4, Kt—K B 3; 2. Kt—Q B 3, P—K Kt 3; 3. P—K 4, P—Q 3; 4. P—Q 4, B—Kt 2; 5. P—B 3, O—O; 6. B—K 3, P—K 4; 7. P—Q 5, Kt—R 4; 8. Q—Q 2, P—K B 4; 9. P × P, P × P; 10. O—O—O, Kt—Q 2; 11. Kt—R 3, Kt(Q 2)—B 3; 12. B—Kt 5, Q—K 1; 13. B—Q 3, Q—B 2.

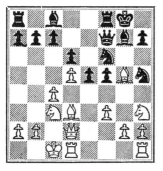

*

14. K R—Kt 1

2 points. In this variation of the King's Indian Defence White castles Q R and aims at breaking open lines for attack on the king's side. Here two methods of carrying out this plan seem to be available: the advance P—K B 4 and the advance P—K Kt 4. The preference for P—K Kt 4 is justified partly because it will include an attack on the exposed black knight, and partly because if Black as in this game, counters with ... P—B 5; White will have the central square K 4 available for occupation. 2 points for 14 Kt—B 2 or 14. Q R—Kt 1, with the same intention as the text.

14. ...   P—B 3

*

15. Q R—B 1

3 points. Now P—K Kt 4 is already threatened, owing to the concealed pin on the K B file. Deduct a point for the positional blunder 15. P × P ?, P × P; when Black has excellent chances owing to the open Q Kt file, the mobile centre pawn majority, and the object of attack in White's Q B P. Of course, if now 15. ... P × P; 16. P × P, Kt × P ? ?; 17. B—Q B 4.

15. ...   P—B 5

*

16. Kt—B 2

1 point. Deduct 4 points for 16. P—K Kt 4 ?, P × P e.p.

16. ...   P × P

*

17. P × P

1 point.

17. ...   Q—B 2

*

18. P—K Kt 4

2 points.

18. ...   P × P e.p.

*

19. P × P

1 point.

19. ...   B—Q 2

53

If 19 ... Kt × Q P; 20. B × P ch, K × B; 21. Q × Kt (threatening R—R 1) with a winning attack.

*

20. K—Kt 1

3 points. White must be careful, for the impatient 20. P—K Kt 4? (deduct a point), Kt—B 5; 21. B × Kt(B 4), P × B; 22. Q × P?, Kt × Q P; makes *Black's* attack overwhelming! If 20. P—B 4 (no credit) Black could also take over control of the game by the sacrifice 20. ... P—K 5!; 21. Kt × P, Kt × Kt; 22. B × Kt, Q R—B 1. Generally speaking in this variation, White must take great care not to allow the black K B a free diagonal.

20. ...   P—Kt 4

*

21. R—B 1

1 point. White is held up for the moment on the king's side, so turns his attention to the other wing in the hope of making use of the open Q B file. However, 21. B—R 6 (3 points) was the more consistent way of making progress.

21. ...   Q—Kt 3

*

22. B—K 3

2 points for this or 22. B—R 6.

22. ...   Q—Kt 2

*

23. B—R 6

1 point.

23. ...   R—B 2

*

24. R—Kt 2

3 points. Now stronger than 24. B × B (1 point) since he hopes to embarrass the black knight on K R 4.

24. ...   Kt—K 1

*

25. R—R 2

3 points. The advantage of this over 25. R—R 1 (2 points) is that it baits a trap: 25. ... Kt × P; 26. B × P ch!, K × B; 27. B × B dis. ch, K × B; 28. Q—Kt 5 ch, K—B 1; 29. R—R 8 mate.

25. ...   Kt(R 4)—B 3

*

26. P—K Kt 4

2 points. White resumes his full-scale king's side attack. There is still no hurry for 26. B × B (1 point), since 26. ... B × B; 27. Q × B only strengthens White's chances, while Black can still less permit 26. ... B—R 1; 27. Q—Kt 5 ch.

26. ...   Kt—B 2

*

27. P—Kt 5

3 points. Nothing if you protected the Q P, since Black cannot now reply 27. ... Kt(B 3) × P; 28. Kt × Kt, Kt × Kt; 29. B—K 4, B—K 3; 30. R—Q 1. 2 points for 27. R—Kt 1.

27. ...   Kt—K 1

*

28. P—Kt 6

4 points. Opening another file—Black's position is now critical. 1 point only for 28 R—Kt 1, after

which Black can put up a better resistance by 28. ... B—B 4.

28. ...   P × P

*

29. B × K Kt P

1 point.

29. ...   B—B 4 ch

*

30. B × B

1 point.

30. ...   R × B

*

31. R—Kt 1

2 points.

31. ...   R—Q 1

*

32. B × B

2 points. 2 points also for 32. R(R 2)—Kt 2.

32. ...   Kt × B

*

33. R × Kt ch

4 points for this, but 7 points for the forced mating finish 33. R—R 8 ch!, K—B 2 (33. ... K × R; 34. Q—R 6 ch, and mate next move); 34. R × Kt ch!, K × R; 35. Q—R 6 ch, K—B 2; 36. Q—

R 7 ch, K—B 3; 37. Kt—K 4 mate.

33. ...   K × R

*

34. Q—R 6 ch

1 point.

34. ...   K—B 2

*

35. Q—R 7 ch

1 point.

35. ...   K—K 1

If 35. ... K—B 3; 36. Kt—K 4 mate.

*

36. Q × R

1 point.

Black resigns.

Summary: The theme of this game is the technique of a king's side attack which involves the opening of files into the enemy position. If you did badly on this game, it probably indicates that you did not sufficiently concentrate on carrying through White's main plan, but became diverted into looking for opportunities in other parts of the board.

Game No. 18

IN this game you have White. Your consultation partner is Raaphi Persitz, the young Israeli student who did very well in English tournaments during his three years at Oxford University. Your opponent is Galula, of France. The game was played in the World Students' Team Championship at Uppsala, 1956.

The first moves are 1. P—K 4, P—Q B 4; 2. Kt—K B 3, Kt—Q B 3; 3. P—Q 4, P × P; 4. Kt × P, P—K Kt 3; 5. Kt—Q B 3; B—Kt 2; 6. B—K 3, P—Q 3; 7. Q—Q 2, P—K R 4.

*

8. P—B 3

2 points for this or 8. O—O—O. White safeguards his Q B from exchange by an eventual ... Kt—K Kt 5. Nothing for 8. P—B 4, Kt—B 3; 9. P—K R 3 (else 9. ... Kt—K Kt 5), P—R 5!; and Black can aim for the occupation of the square K Kt 6.

8. ...   Kt—B 3

*

9. O—O—O

2 points. The decision as to which side to castle is one which gives some players great difficulty. White's choice is an indication that his subsequent attacking plans will allow for operations either on the K side, if Black castles on that wing, or in the centre, if the black king is left there. The possibility of Black castling Q R can be discounted in view of the absence of a Q B P in the castled king's position.

9. ...   B—Q 2

*

10. B—K 2

1 point. Solid, but 10. B—Q B 4 (3 points) is more aggressive. Nothing for 10. Kt × Kt, B × Kt; since exchanges free Black's position.

10. ...   P—R 3

*

11. Kt—Q 5

2 points. White exploits the new weakness created by Black's last move. The threat is 12. K Kt × Kt, followed by B—Kt 6 and Kt—B 7 ch.

11. ...   K Kt × Kt

*

12. P × Kt

1 point.

12. ...   Kt—K 4

56

*
13. P—K R 3

2 points. Black's centralized knight is his only well-placed piece so White prepares to dislodge it immediately. Nothing for 13. P—K B 4, Kt—Kt 5; 14. B—Kt 1, since the knight can retreat to a useful square at K B 3.

13. ...   Q—B 1

*
14. P—Q Kt 3

1 point. The same motif as on the previous move.

14. ...   P—B 4

*
15. P—K B 4

1 point. Now that Black's knight is driven back to a square whence it has little scope, this move is in order.

15. ...   Kt—B 2

*
16. P—K Kt 4

4 points. This break-through is the logical culmination of White's previous strategy. Black's rooks are not connected, his queen is badly placed, and his K 3 is weak. White, on the other hand, has a strong grip on the centre, and the opening of the position can only favour his well-placed minor pieces.

16. ...   R P × P

*
17. P × P

1 point.

17. ...   Kt—R 3

If 17. ... P × P; 18. R × R ch, followed by R—R 1, is very strong.

*
18. P—Kt 5

2 points. 18 P × P? (no credit), Kt × P; would allow Black's pieces the use of an important central square. It might be argued that the text-move leaves White only one file on which to attack, but in this case not only is there a sure entry-point at K R 7, but White can reasonably expect the K file to be opened up also.

18. ...   Kt—B 2

*
19. R × R ch

2 points. There is no way of preparing to double rooks on the K R file.

19. ...   B × R

*
20. R—R 1

1 point.

20. ...   B—Kt 2

*
21. R—R 7

1 point.

21. ...   K—B 1

*
22. Kt—K 6 ch

7 points. This pawn sacrifice allows White's queen and bishops to join in the attack with decisive effect. For readers who feel hesitant at sacrificing material unless they see a clear and immediate win, it should be pointed out that

no other move helps the attack.
Both 22. B—B 4 and 22. P—B 4
are answered by 22. ... P—Q Kt 4,
while 22. Q—K 1, followed by
Q—R 1, does not enable White to
extend his break-through on the
K R file. A master would not
normally work out all the consequences of Kt—K 6 ch; it would
be enough for him to foresee that
both his bishops could be directed
to diagonals bearing on the black
king.

22. ...   B × Kt
*
23. P × B
1 point.
23. ...   Q × P
*
24. B—B 4
2 points.
24. ...   Q—B 1
*
25. B—Q 4
5 points. Less good is 25. B ×
Kt (no credit), K × B; 26. B—
Q 4 (26. Q—Q 5 ch, P—K 3),
P—K 4; 27. P × P, K—Kt 1!;
28. R × B ch, K × R; 29. P—K 6
dis. ch, K—B 1!; 30. Q—R 2, K—
K 2!; and Black escapes. 2 points
for 25. Q—Q 5, P—K 3; 26. Q × K P,
when White should win the ending,
although Black can resist for much
longer than after the text.
25. ...   P—K 4

*
26. P × P
1 point.
26. ...   P × P
*
27. B × K P
5 points. If now 27. ... Kt × B;
28. Q—Q 6 ch, and wins.
27. ...   B × B
*
28. R × Kt ch
1 point.
28. ...   K—K 1
*
29. Q—Kt 4
3 points.
Black resigns.

Summary: Sometimes you find
your opponent eschewing active
counterplay and setting up a
purely defensive position in which,
in effect, he challenges you to
'come and get him'. In such
positions, many players attack
without sufficient preparation,
others do not make use of their
opponents' lack of counterplay.
This game and game No. 31
(Flohr-Frydman) are models of
the treatment of this type of
situation, and if you did badly on
these two games you should study
them carefully.

Game No. 19

IN this game you have Black. Your consultation partner is Iceland's young star Fridrijk Olafsson. Your opponent is Bert Larsen, Danish champion. The game was played in the match for the Scandinavian Championship, 1956. The first moves are 1. Kt—K B 3, P—K B 4; 2. P—K Kt 3, Kt—K B 3; 3. B—Kt 2, P—K 3; 4. O—O, B—K 2; 5. P—B 4, O—O; 6. P—Q 4, P—Q 3; 7. Kt—B 3, Q—K 1; 8. P—Kt 3, P—Q R 4; 9. B—Kt 2, Kt—R 3; 10. P—Q R 3, B—Q 2; 11. Kt—K 1.

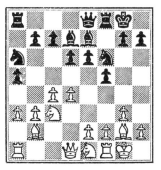

*

11. ...   P—B 3

2 points. In the Dutch Defence with ... P—Q 3; Black normally aims at an early central advance with ... P—K 4; and the present move shields his Q 4 from any subsequent occupation by White's pieces. Deduct a point for 11. ... B—B 3?; 12. P—Q 5, P × P; 13. Kt × P, with much the better game for White, and take no

credit for the passive 11. ... R Kt 1.

12. Kt—Q 3

*

12. ...   B—Q 1

2 points. Still preparing for ... P—K 4 and at the same time allowing the bishop to be transferred to a more aggressive diagonal at Q B 2 or Q Kt 3.

13. P—K 4

*

13. ...   P—K 4

3 points. It must be now or never, for if 13. ... P × P (no credit); 14. Kt × P, White's Q B acts an extra deterrent to ... P—K 4.

14. Q P × P

*

14. ...   Q P × P

1 point.

15. Q—K 2

*

15. ...   P—B 5

8 points. This is the kind of move which always seems to be logically compelling when played by a master, yet if we are confronted with the possibility in our own games we shrink from it because the consequences seem so indefinite. So let us analyse Black's motives for this move.

1. White threatens to win a good pawn by simply 16. P × P and 17. Q × P or 17. Kt × P.

59

2. Black sees that if he avoids losing a pawn by the obvious manœuvre 15. ... P × P; 16. Q Kt × P (threatening 17. Kt—Q 6), B—B 2; then 17. Kt(Q 3)—B 5!, Kt(B 3) × Kt; 18. Kt × Kt(K 4), and with an unassailable outpost at K 4, White can already look forward to occupying the Q file and invading at Q 6.

3. Again, if simply 15. ... B—B 2; then 16. P × P, B × P; 17. Kt—K 4, and again White has the annoying central strongpoint with its favourable outlooks on Q B 5 and Q 6.

4. So Black looks round for some way of denying White this valuable square at K 4. He probably did not consider ... P—B 5 till this stage, but now would note the following advantages:

A. White's K 4 remains blocked by a pawn.

B. Black's own K 4 square can become a manœuvring-point for his pieces.

C. Both Black's bishops will obtain excellent diagonals and can be directed against White's king.

D. The white king will lose one of its protecting barrier of pawns.

All in all, then, 15. ... P—B 5 begins to appear the most logical move; and, generally speaking, most masters prefer to be a pawn behind with active counterplay rather than be tied down to completely passive defence which, in the long run, is the more certain cause of defeat.

16 P × P

*

16. ...   P × P

1 point.

17. Kt × P

*

17. ...   Kt—B 4

2 points for this, which brings the Q Kt into action. 17. ... Kt—K Kt 5 (no credit) looks promising, but does not lead to anything definite after 18. Kt—Q 3 (18. ... Q—R 4?; 19. P—R 3). Or if 17. ... B—B 2; 18. Kt—Q 3.

18. Q R—Q 1

*

18. ...   B—B 2

4 points. Deduct 2 points for the greedy 18. ... Kt × Kt P; when White obtains excellent counterplay with 19. P—K 5!, Kt—Kt 5; 20. P—K 6!, R × Kt; 21. P × B. That the passed pawn is now guarded by the rook at Q 1 explains White's 18th move.

19. P—Kt 4

(If 19. Kt—Q 3, Kt × Kt P; 20. P—K 5, Kt—Kt 5; favours Black, as 21. P—K 6 is no longer possible.)

*

19. ...   P × P

2 points. There is certainly no harm in opening another file.

20. P × P

*

20. ...   B × Kt

3 points. This is much stronger than retreating the knight (deduct 1 point), since White then safeguards himself with 21. Kt—Q 3.

21. P × Kt

*

21. ...   B—Kt 5

4 points. Still better than 21 ....
Kt—Kt 5 (2 points).

22. P—B 3

*

22. ...   Q—R 4

8 points. A well-calculated final
combination. If 23. P × B, Q ×
R P ch; 24. K—B 2, Q—R 5 ch;
25. K—Kt 1, B—R 7 ch; 26. K—
R 1, B—Kt 6 ch; and wins.

23. B—K R 1

*

23. ...   Q × B P ch

4 points.

24. K—Kt 2

*

24. ...   B—R 6 ch

6 points. White resigns, for if
25. K × B, Q—R 4 ch; 26. K—
Kt 2, Q × P mate.

Summary: White's slow manœuvring (particularly the time-
consuming regrouping of the
knight on moves 11 and 12)
enabled Black to prepare a king's
side attack, the theme of which
was the weakness of White's K R 2
(no longer protected by the
knight!). The move 15. ... P—B 5,
which was much the most difficult
in the game, must have been discovered partly by consideration of
this factor and partly by Black's
realization that any other continuation would tie him permanently
to the defence of a weak K P.
Masters do not reject cramped
positions as such; but generally
speaking, an active game a pawn
down is much preferable to a
position with level material where
you are bound to the defence of a
positional weakness.

Game No. 20

In this game you have White. Your consultation partner is the Russian grandmaster Alexander Kotov. Your opponent is G. Bastrikov. The game was played in the semi-final of the Russian Championship at Erevan, 1954. The first moves are 1. P—Q 4, Kt—K B 3; 2. P—Q B 4, P—K 3; 3. Kt—Q B 3, P—B 4; 4. P—Q 5, P × P; 5. P × P, P—Q 3; 6. P—K 4, B—K 2; 7. B—Q 3, O—O; 8. Kt—B 3, B—Kt 5; 9. P—K R 3, B—R 4.

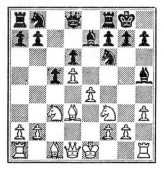

*

10. P—K Kt 4

2 points. With a good share of the centre, White can confidently make this advance to emphasize Black's error in avoiding ... B × Kt last move. 1 point for 10. O—O or 10. B—K B 4.

10. ...   B—Kt 3

*

11. Kt—Q 2

2 points. Again the sharpest continuation; the unfortunate bishop is to be further harassed by the advance of the K B P,

while in some circumstances the white K Kt may find a good square at Q B 4. Nothing for the routine 11. B—K B 4 or 11. O—O, and deduct 2 points for 11. Kt—K R 4?, B × P!

11. ...   K Kt—Q 2

*

12. P—B 4

1 point.

12. ...   P—B 3

*

13. O—O

1 point. 13. P—B 5? (deduct 1 point) would be a positional error because Black could reply 13. ... Kt—K 4! and maintain a knight on this central outpost, but 13. Kt—B 3 or 13. Kt—B 4 (1 point each) are adequate alternatives.

13. ...   R—K 1

*

14. P—Kt 3

1 point for this, Kt—B 4 or Kt—B 3.

14. ...   Kt—R 3

*

15. B—Kt 2

1 point for this, Kt—B 4 or Kt—B 3.

15. ...   Kt—B 2

*

16. Q—B 3

3 points. This brings the queen into the attack, and is more imaginative than Kt—B 4, Kt—B 3, P—Q R 4, or P—K R 4 (1 point each).

16. ...   Q—Kt 1

*

17. P—Q R 4

2 points for this; nothing for other moves, since Black threatens counterplay with ... P—Kt 4.

17. ...   P—Q R 3

*

18. P—R 4

1 point. 1 point for 18. P—R 5 which can also be played, although after the text 18. ... P—Q Kt 4 costs a pawn.

18. ...   P—R 3

*

19. Q—R 3

3 points for this, which threatens the immediate 20. P—Kt 5, breaking through and at the same time attacking the knight.

19. ...   Kt—B 1

*

20. R—B 2

2 points. Again there is plenty of reasonable choice in this position, indicating that the difficulty in this type of situation is not to find good *moves* but to decide upon the best *formation* which will enable the eventual breakthrough to take place with maximum effect. 2 points for 20. K—R 1, 20. Kt—B 3, 20. P—B 5, 20. Kt—K 2, or 20. Q R—K 1.

20. ...   P—Kt 3

*

21. Kt—K 2

2 points, and 2 points for 21. R—Kt 2, 21. Q R—K B 1, 21. R—K 1, 21. P—B 5, and 21. Kt—B 3.

21. ...   Q—B 1.

*

22. P—B 5

1 point and 1 point for 22. R—Kt 2, 22. Q R—K B 1, and 22. Kt—K B 3.

22. ...   B—B 2

*

23. Kt—K B 3

1 point for this, 23. Q R—K B 1, 23. R—Kt 2, and 23. Kt—K B 4.

23. ...   Kt—R 2

*

24. Kt—B 4

1 point for this or 24. R—Kt 2.

24. ...   P—Q Kt 4

*

25. P—Q R 5

3 points. With all his pieces concentrated on the king's side, White naturally prefers to keep the other wing completely closed.

25. ...   Q—Kt 2

*

26. B—B 2

1 point for this, 26. K—R 1, 26. R—Kt 2, or 26. Q R—K B 1.

26. ...   K R—Q B 1

*

27. R—Kt 2

1 point for this or 27. K—R 1.

27. ...   Kt—K 1

*

28. P—Kt 5

6 points. Note how White took every precaution before finally embarking on this break-through, even to withdrawing his bishop

63

from Q 3 so as to deprive the counter-attack ... P—B 5 of any significance.

28. ...   B P × P

*

29. P × P

1 point.

29. ...   Kt × P

*

30. Kt × Kt

1 point.

30. ...   B × Kt

*

31. R × B

3 points. This sacrifice is an essential part of the break-through combination.

31. ...   P × R

*

32. Kt—Kt 6

2 points.

32. ...   B × Kt

*

33. P × B

1 point.

33. ...   Kt—B 3

*

34. Q—K 6 ch

3 points. Deduct 1 point for 34. B × Kt?, P × B; 35. Q—K 6 ch, K—Kt 2; when White has good losing chances. Now if 34. ... K—R 1; 35. K—Kt 2.

34. ...   K—B 1

*

35. B × Kt

1 point.

35. ...   P × B

*

36. R—K B 1

3 points.

Black resigns.

The finish might be 36. ... K—Kt 2; 37. Q × P ch, K—Kt 1; 38. Q—K 6 ch, K—R 1; 39. R—B 2.

Summary: Compare this game with Nos. 18 and 31 as regards its illustration of how to attack a cramped position. White does not make his final break-through until all his pieces are on the best possible squares for taking advantage of it.

Game No. 21

IN this game you have White. Your consultation partner is Peter Clarke, the 23-year-old Essex player who was one of the heroes of the British team in the International team tournament at Moscow, 1956, where he was unbeaten. Your opponent is Roman Toran, Spain's strongest master. The game was played in the Hastings tournament, 1956-7. The first moves are 1. P—K 4, P—Q B 4; 2. Kt—K B 3, P—Q 3; 3. P—Q 4, P × P; 4. Kt × P, Kt—K B 3; 5. Kt—Q B 3, P—Q R 3; 6. P—B 4, P—K 4; 7. Kt—B 3, Q Kt—Q 2.

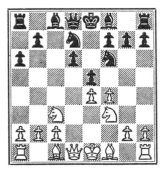

*

8. B—B 4

2 points. 2 points also for 8. B—Q 3, but only 1 for 8. B—K 2 (after which 8. ... P—Q Kt 4, followed by ... B—Kt 2; puts White's K P under attack), and none for 8. P × P, P × P; when Black's K B can occupy a fine diagonal at Q B 4.

8. ...   B—K 2

Black should contest the control of his Q 4 square by 8. ... Q—B 2; 9. Q—K 2, P—Q Kt 4; 10. B—Q 5, B—Kt 2.

*

9. P—Q R 4

3 points. Part of White's plan is to prevent Black from obtaining a queen's side initiative by ... P—Q Kt 4. 1 point for 9. O—O or 9. Q—K 2, but nothing for 9. B—K 3, when Black causes trouble by 9. ... Kt—Kt 5; 10. B—Q 2, Q—Kt 3.

9. ...   O—O

10. Q—K 2

3 points. Here 10. O—O (1 point) would be less convincing as there is no clear compensation for the pawn after 10. ... P × P; 11. B × B P, Q—Kt 3 ch; 12. K—R 1, Q × P. 10. P × P (1 point) still releases the tension in the centre at an unduly early stage, while 10. P—B 5. (no credit), with the strategical object of strengthening the grip on the white squares, would be tactically upset by 10. ... Kt—B 4; 11. Q—K 2, Q Kt × K P; 12. Kt × Kt, P—Q 4.

10. ...   P—Q Kt 3

A second passive and bad move. He should strive for counterplay by 10. ... P × P; 11. B × B P, Kt—B 4; 12. O—O, B—K 3.

*

11. O—O

2 points.

11. ...   B—Kt 2

65

12. P × P

3 points. No credit for 12. Kt—Q 5, Kt × Kt; 13. B × Kt, B × B; 14. P × B, since the square Q 5 is useful to White only as a focal point for piece manœuvres, and must not be blocked by a pawn. 12. P—B 5 (1 point) is playable, but White considers that, in view of the strongly posted bishop at Q B 4, he can do still better by opening the K B file and attacking Black's K B 2. 12. B—K 3 (no credit) permits Black to free his game by 12. ... Kt—Kt 5; 13. B—Q 2, P × P; 14. B × B P, Kt(Kt 5)—K 4.

12. ...   P × P

*

13. B—K Kt 5

3 points. White is still thinking in terms of controlling his Q 5, and so this move is preferable to 13. B—K 3 (1 point), when Black can make the freeing exchange 13. ... B—B 4. Other moves like 13. K—R 1 (no credit) give Black too much time to improve his game.

13. ...   Kt—R 4

*

14. Q R—Q 1

5 points. A finely calculated move which takes advantage of the insecurity of Black's piece formation. If now 14. ... B × B; 15. Kt × B, Kt—B 5; 16. K R × Kt, P × R; 17. Q—R 5, Kt—B 3; 18. B × P ch, K—R 1; 19. R × Q, Kt × Q; 20. R × R ch, R × R; 21. B × Kt, winning a piece,

while if 14. ... B × B; 15. Kt × B, Kt (R 4)—B 3; 16. K R × Kt, P × R; 17. Kt × R P, K × Kt; 18. Q—R 5 ch, K—Kt 2; 19. Q—Kt 4 ch, followed by R—Q 3 and wins.

Only 1 point for 14. B × B, Q × B; threatening ... Kt—B 5; and nothing for 14. B—K 3, B—B 4 (again threatening ... Kt—B 5). Deduct 2 points for the blunder 14. P—R 4, Kt—Kt 6.

14. ...   B—B 4 ch

*

15. K—R 1

2 points. Nothing for 15. B—K 3, Kt—B 5.

15. ...   Q—B 2

*

16. R × Kt

9 points. This well-calculated sacrifice wins by force. 4 points for 16. Kt—Q 5, which is good enough for a clear positional advantage, as is 16. B—Q 5 (3 points). Against other moves, Black can ease his position by blocking the K B file with 16. ... Kt—B 5.

16. ...   Q × R

*

17. Kt × P

2 points.

17. ...   Q—B 2

*

18. Kt × P

2 points. Less convincing is 18. Q × Kt, Q × Kt; 19. R × P, R × R; 20. B × R ch, K—R 1; 21. B—Kt 6, P—R 3.

66

18. ...   P—Kt 3

The only move to avoid immediate loss, for if 18. ... Kt—B 3; 19. B × Kt, P × B; 20. Q—Kt 4 mate.

*

19. Kt—Q 5

6 points. While the immediate discovered checks by the knight lead to nothing decisive, this move leaves Black without resource. Besides his actual reply, Black can only try 19. ... Q—Kt 1; where 20. Kt—B 6 ch, Kt × Kt; 21. B × Kt; leaves him helpless against the threatened 22. Kt—R 6 mate, e.g. 21. ... R × Kt; 22. B × R ch, K × B; 23. B—K 5 dis. ch. or 21. ... P—K R 4; 22. Kt—Kt 5 dis. ch.

19. ...   B × Kt

*

20. B × B

2 points.

20. ...   R—R 2

*

21. Kt—Q 6 dis. ch.

3 points.

21. ...   K—Kt 2

*

22. R × R

3 points. Black resigns, for if 22. ... K × R; 23. Q—B 3 ch, K—Kt 2; 24. Kt—K 8 ch, winning the queen.

Summary: White's control of important files (the Q and K B files) and an equally important diagonal (from Q R 2 to K Kt 8) enabled him to launch a powerful attack, and the combinations which followed were also based on his possession of these open lines. In other words, play well positionally and the tactical fruits will come. If you did play badly on this game it may mean that you did not pay sufficient attention to White's basic plan, or alternatively that you did not properly calculate the effects of the sacrificial concepts in the later stages.

Game No. 22

IN this game you have White. Your consultation partner is Alexander Tolush, one of the most brilliant combinative players of today. Your opponent is V. Antoshin. The game was played in the 1957 Russian Championship.
The first moves are 1. P—K 4, P—K 3; 2. P—Q 4, P—Q 4; 3. Kt —Q B 3, B—Kt 5; 4. P—K 5, Q—Q 2; 5. P—Q R 3, B × Kt ch; 6. P × B, P—Q Kt 3; 7. Q—Kt 4, P—K B 4; 8. Q—Kt 3, B—R 3; 9. B × B, Kt × B.

*

10. Kt—K 2

2 points for this or for 10. Kt— R 3. White's knight heads for its natural outpost at K B 4, whence it is directed against the base of Black's pawn chain. 1 point only for the routine move 10. Kt—B 3. Nothing for the positional blunder 10. P—K B 4, which takes away the best square from the knight and hems in White's own bishop. Nothing for moves of the bishop or 10. P—Q R 4, since it is not yet

clear on which side of the board the bishop will have more scope.

10. ...   Kt—Kt 1

*

11. Kt—B 4

1 point.

11. ...   Q—B 2

*

12. P—Q B 4

2 points for this ingenious idea, which aims at securing a tremendous attack at the price of two pawns after 12. ... P × P; 13. P—Q 5, P × P; 14. B—Kt 2, but 4 points for 12. Kt × K P!, after which the main variation runs 12. ... Q × Kt; 13. Q × P, Q— Kt 3; 14. Q × R, Kt—Q 2; 15. P—K R 4!, O—O—O; 16. P— R 5, Q—B 2; 17. P—R 6, Kt × R P; 18. Q × R ch, K × Q; 19. R × Kt, and White should win.

12. ...   Kt—K 2

*

13. P × P

1 point. White's plan has at any rate eliminated the doubled pawn so characteristic of this variation.

13. ...   Kt × P

*

14. Kt—K 2

3 points. Although White's bishop would have the run of the black squares after 14. Kt × Kt (1 point), P × Kt; White's pawns would remain immobile and it would not be at all easy for him to break through. After the move

actually played, White threatens P—Q B 4 and an eventual P—Q 5, so that Black is virtually obliged to weaken his pawns.

14. ...   P—Q Kt 4

*

15. Q—Kt 3

2 points for this or 15. R—Q Kt 1. White at once seizes on the weakness. 1 point for 15. P—Q R 4, which is also strong. Nothing for 15. O—O; as will be seen, White's immediate action on the Q Kt file has a combinational point.

15. ...   Q—Q 2

*

16. R—Q Kt 1

1 point.

16. ...   P—B 3

*

17. P—Q R 4

3 points. This is very strong here since Black cannot answer 17. ... P—Kt 5; 18. P—Q B 4, P × P e.p.; because of 19. Q × Kt ch, winning a piece. Equally strong here is 17. P—Q B 4 (3 points).

17. ...   P—Q R 3

*

18. P—Q B 4

1 point.

18. ...   Kt—Kt 3

*

19. R P × P

1 point for this or 19. B P × P. The win of a pawn is of no great significance in itself; what counts is that White's bishop now obtains a fine diagonal.

19. ...   R P × P

*

20. P × P

1 point.

20. ...   O—O

*

21. B—R 3

3 points for this, but nothing for 21. P × P, which only develops Black after 21. ... Kt × P (22. Q × Kt?, Q R—Kt 1).

21. ...   R—Q 1

*

22. B—B 5

3 points. Although White is a good pawn up, further progress would become difficult if Black could establish his knight on Q 4. Thus, no credit for 22. Kt—B 4, Kt—Q 4; 23. Kt × Kt, Q × Kt; (threatening Q × Q and P × P); 24. Q × Q, R × Q; regaining the pawn; and nothing for 22. B—Q 6 (P × P; 23. Q × P??, Q × Q; 24. R × Q, R—R 8 ch). Now, however, White can reply to 22. ... Kt—Q 4 by 23. P—Kt 6, with an overwhelmingly strong passed pawn, and to 22. ... P × P; by 23. B × Kt.

22. ...   Kt—R 5

*

23. B—Q 6

1 point.

23. ...   R—R 4

*

24. O—O

3 points. A great attacking player like Tolush often prefers to have a lasting initiative rather than an extra pawn which is hard to

69

evaluate, and this is why this move is preferred to 24. P × P (3 points). Nothing for 24. Kt—B 4?, R × P; or for 24. P—Kt 6, R—Kt 4; 25. Q—B 2, Kt × P.

24. ...   P × P

*

25. Kt—B 4

2 points. First Black's rook is tied to passive defence . . .

25. ...   R—K 1

*

26. P—Q 5

3 points. White opens yet another line of attack. 3 points also for 26. K R—B 1.

26. ...   P × P

*

27. K R—B 1

2 points for this or 27. Q × P ch. 27. Kt × P, Q—K B 2; allows a stiffer resistance.

27. ...   Kt—Kt 3

*

28. R—B 7

1 point.

28. ...   Q—Q 1

*

29. Q—Q B 3

3 points. 29. Q—Kt 3 (3 points), Kt(1)—Q 2; 30. P—K 6 also wins quickly, but the text is prettier.

29. ...   R—R 5

(If 29. ... Kt—B 5; 30. Q—K Kt 3, Kt—Q 2; 31. Kt—R 5, P—Kt 3; 32. R × Kt (Q 7)!).

*

30. R × P ch

5 points for this brilliant concluding combination. If now 30. ...

K—R 1; 31. P—K 6, Q × B (31. ... P—Q 5; 32. B—K 5!); 32. R—K 7 dis. ch., P—Q 5; 33. R × R ch, K—Kt 2; 34. Q—Kt 3 ch, forcing mate.

30. ...   K × R

*

31. P—K 6 dis. ch.

1 point.

31. ...   K—R 3

*

32. Q—R 3 ch

1 point.

32. ...   K—Kt 2

*

33. B—K 5 ch

2 points.

Black resigns, for he is mated after 33. ... K—Kt 1; 34. Q—Kt 3 ch, K—B 1; 35. Q—Kt 7, or 33. ... K—B 1; 34. Q—R 6 ch, K—K 2; 35. Q—B 6 mate.

Summary: The theme of this game is the dynamic activity of White's pieces, which far outweighs the static quality of the pawns he sacrifices. If you did badly, it probably indicates that, if you win material, you tend to play too passively in your efforts to retain this advantage, and do not look hard enough for opportunities of returning the material in order to obtain a winning attack or a decisive endgame plus. As a remedy, make a habit of looking out specially for such opportunities whenever you are materially ahead but feel you are gradually losing the initiative.

V   THE ART OF DEFENCE

Game No. 23

IN this game you have White. Your consultation partner is Lothar Schmid, one of Germany's best players. Your opponent is A. Barth. The game was played in Dresden, 1947.

The first moves are 1. P—K 4, P—K 4; 2. Kt—K B 3, Kt—Q B 3; 3. B—Kt 5, P—Q R 3; 4. B—R 4, Kt—B 3; 5. O—O, B—K 2; 6. R—K 1, P—Q Kt 4; 7. B—Kt 3, P—Q 3; 8. P—B 3, B—Kt 5; 9. P—Q 3, O—O; 10. Q Kt—Q 2, P—Q 4 ; 11. P—K R 3, B—R 4.

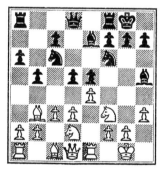

*

12. P × P

2 points for this or 12. P—K Kt 4. Nothing for 12. Kt—B 1 ?, P × P; 13. P × P, Q × Q; 14. R × Q, B × Kt; when White has mediocre prospects owing to his wrecked pawns.

12. ...   Kt × P

*

13. P—K Kt 4

2 points for this; only 1 for 13. Kt—B 1. White can win the pawn, although it takes masterly defence to prove it.

13. ...   B—Kt 3

*

14. Kt × P

1 point.

14. ...   Kt × Kt

*

15. R × Kt

1 point.

15. ...   Kt—B 5

*

16. Kt—K 4

5 points. Nothing for 16. Q—B 3, trying to hold everything, when a game Barth-Schmid, 1944 (the same players with colours reversed!) continued 16. ... Kt × P; 17. R—Q 5, B—Q 3!; 18. Kt—B 1, P—Q B 3; 19. R—Q 4, P—Q B 4 ; 20. R—Q 5, P—B 5; 21. B—Q 1, Q—K 2; 22. Kt—Kt 3, B × Kt; 23. P × B, Q—K 8 ch; Resigns.

16. ...   Kt × P ch

*

17. K—Kt 2

3 points. Deduct 2 points for 17. K—R 2, B × Kt; and deduct

71

4 points for 17. K—R 1 ??, B ×
Kt ch.

17. ...   B × Kt ch

*
18. P × B

2 points. Not 18. R × B?
(deduct 1 point), Kt—Kt 4; when
the knight escapes.

18. ...   B—Q 3

*
19. R—Q 5

3 points. Sharper than 19. R—
K B 5 (2 points), P—Kt 3; 20.
R × P, R × R; 21. B × R ch,
K × B; 22. K × Kt, although
this should also win in the long
run. Deduct 3 points for 19. R—
R 5?, Kt—B 5 ch; when again the
knight escapes and Black has
much the superior game.

19. ...   Kt × P

An ingenious resource; if instead 19. ... Q—R 5; 20. Q—B 3,
Kt × P?; 21. R—R 5.

*
20. K × Kt

3 points. This is sufficient to
win, but from the practical point
of view, 20. Q—B 3 (6 points) is
simpler, since the errant knight
then has no escape.

20. ...   Q—R 5 ch

*
21. K—K 3

5 points. White must run to the
queen's side to escape perpetual
check.

21. ...   Q R—K 1

*
22. Q—B 3

6 points. Not 22. B—Q 2? (no
credit), Q—Kt 6 ch; 23. Q—B 3,
R × P ch!; 24. K × R, R—
K 1 ch; nor 22. K—Q 3? (no
credit), Q—Kt 6 ch; 23. B—K 3,
B—B 5; 24. Q—K 2, R × P!

22. ...   Q—K 8 ch

*
23. K—Q 3

3 points. Not 23. Q—K 2?
(deduct 3 points), R × P ch.

23. ...   R—K 2

Admitting that his attack is
inadequate.

*
24. R × B

4 points. White wins more
material.

24. ...   P × R

*
25. B—Kt 5

2 points.

25. ...   Q × R

*
26. B × R

1 point.

26. ...   R—B 1

*
27. Q × P ch

1 point.

27. ...   K—R 1

*
28. B—B 8

3 points.

Black resigns.

Summary: White's acceptance of the proffered material was based on his confidence in his own superior development, but this would have been useless had not White calculated accurately all the possibilities when his king was drawn into the centre and made sure that he could find safety on the queen's side. If you went wrong on moves 16, 17, 18, 19, 20, or 22, it indicates that you need to rely less on general judgments in complicated positions and should make greater efforts to work out the exact consequences of each move.

73

Game No. 24

In this game you have Black. Your consultation partner is Salo Flohr, who throughout his career has been one of the hardest players in the world to defeat. Your opponent is Ladislav Alster of Czechoslovakia. The game was played in the Marianske Lazne tournament, 1956.

The first moves are 1. P—K 4, P—Q B 4; 2. Kt—K B 3, P—Q R 3; 3. P—Q B 4, Kt—Q B 3; 4. P—Q 4, P × P; 5. Kt × P, Q—B 2; 6. Kt—Q B 3, P—K 3; 7. B—K 3, Kt—B 3; 8. P—Q R 3, P—Q Kt 3; 9. R—B 1, Kt × Kt; 10. B × Kt, B—Kt 2; 11. P—B 3, P—Q 3; 12. B—K 2, B—K 2; 13. O—O, O—O; 14. Q—Q2.

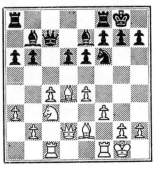

*

14. ...   Kt—Q 2

4 points. This is another 'Maroczy bind' position (see game 10) with the difference that Black's K B is at K 2 instead of being fianchettoed. His counterplay, however, still lies on the black squares, which explains why he prepares to exchange the black-squared bishops. More routine moves like 14. ... Q R—B 1, or 14. ... K R—Q 1 (2 points each) would allow White the choice between a strong attack (15. P—K Kt 4) or queen's side pressure (15. Q—K 3).

15. K R—Q 1

*

15. ...   Q R—B 1

2 points for this or 15. ... K R—Q 1. Deduct 5 points if you didn't notice that the immediate 15. ... B—K B 3? now loses the Q P for nothing.

16. P—Q Kt 4

*

16. ...   Q—Kt 1

3 points for this, 2 points for 16. ... K R—Q 1. White's queen's side advance involves the risk that his pawns may become fixed and weak, and the queen move foreshadows the 'stabilizing operation' ... P—Q Kt 4.

17. P—B 4

*

17. ...   B—Q B 3

2 points. The same motif. 1 point for 17. ... K R—Q 1.

18. Q—Q 3

Preventing 18. ... P—Q Kt 4, so Black reverts to his original plan.

*

18. ...   K R—Q 1

2 points.

19. Q—R 3

*

19. ...   B—B 3

2 points.

20. B × B

*

20. ...   Kt × B

1 point.

21. B—Q 3

*

21. ...   Kt—Q 2

3 points. Many a player would panic at White's coming attack and play some such move as 21. ... P—K R 3 (no credit) when P— K Kt 4-5 is tremendously strong, or 21. ... P—Kt 3 (no credit) when the attack could be successfully continued with 22. P—K Kt 4, followed by Q—R 4 and R— K 1-K 3-R 3.

22. R—B 1

*

22. ...   P—Q Kt 4!

5 points. Note how Black immediately seizes the opportunity of obtaining a point of counter-attack. If 23. P × P, P × P; Black's rooks at once transfer their attentions to the sick Q R P.

23. P—K 5

*

23. ...   Kt—B 1.

3 points. Again Black avoids weakening his pawn front.

24. P—K B 5

*

24. ...   Kt P × P

5 points. Among a bewildering choice of pawn captures this is

clearly the strongest, as is clear from an examination of the alternatives: (1) 24. ... K P × P; 25. B × P, R—B 2; 26. K P × P, R × P; 27. P—B 5, and White's 'weak' queen side pawns are suddenly very powerful. (2) 24. ... Q P × P; 25. P × K P!, B P × P; 26. R × Kt ch!, K × R; 27. R—B 1 ch (not 27. Q × K P, R × B; 28. R—B 1 ch, B—B 6), K—K 1 (27. ... K—K 2; 28. Q—R 4 ch, K— K 1; 29. Q—R 5 ch transposes); 28. Q—R 5 ch, P—Kt 3; 29. B × P ch, P × B; 30. Q × P ch, K— Q 2; 31. Q—B 7 ch, K—Q 3; 32. P—B 5 mate.

25. P × K P

If 25. B × P, Q—Kt 3 ch!; 26. K—R 1, Q—Q 5!; 27. B—Q 3, Q P × P; and the attack is repulsed.

*

25. ...   P × B

1 point.

26. R × P

*

26. ...   R—K 1

3 points. Deduct 2 points for 26. ... B—K 1?; 27. R × Kt ch!, K × R; 28. R—B 1 ch, K—Kt 1 (28. ... K—K 2; 29. Kt—Q 5 mate); 29. P—K 7.

27. R(B 1)—B 1

*

27. ...   Kt × P

2 points. Not 27. ... R × P? (deduct 4 points); 28. R × Kt ch.

28. R(B 1)—B 6

Despair.

75

*

28. ...   Q—Kt 3 ch

3 points.

29. K—R 1

*

29. ...   P × P

2 points. Now if 30. R × Kt, R × R; 31. Q × R, B × P ch.

30. Q—Kt 4

*

30. ...   Q—Q 5

3 points. But not 30. ... B—R 1 (deduct 2 points); 31. R × Kt!

31. Q—R 5

*

31. ...   Q × Kt

1 point. The rewards for Black's patient defence are indeed numerous.

32. P—R 3

*

32. ...   Q—K 8 ch

1 point.

33. K—R 2

*

33. ...   Q—K 7

1 point.

34. R × P ch

*

34. ...   Kt × R

1 point. But deduct 6 points for 34. ... K × R; by which Black could still lose—35. R—B 7 ch.

35. Q—B 7 ch

*

35. ...   K—R 1

No credit for the only legal move! White was in desperate time trouble in the last few moves, which explains his delay in resigning. However, after 36. R—B 2, Q—R 4; 37. Q—B 6, Q—Kt 3; he did so.

Summary: The art of defence is one of the most difficult in chess, not only because of the intrinsic care and avoidance of error required in defensive positions, but also because, psychologically, the inexperienced defender is liable to panic, lose heart or become impatient. For those who scored badly in this game, I recommend a study of the games of Dr. Lasker, who was probably the greatest defensive player of all time. A good edition of his games by J. Gilchrist is available in English.

VI COMBINATIONS

Game No. 25

IN this game you have White. Your consultation partner is German master Kurt Richter, who in his prime was one of the most dangerous attacking players in the world. Your opponent is A. Vogel. The game was played in the Berlin championship, 1952. The first moves are 1. P—K 4, P—Q 3; 2. P—Q 4, Kt—K B 3; 3. Kt—Q B 3, P—K Kt 3; 4. P—K R 4, B—Kt 2; 5. B—K 2, P—K R 4; 6. B—Kt 5, Q Kt—Q 2; 7. Kt—B 3, P—B 3.

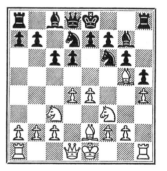

*

8. Q—Q 3

3 points. In sharp attacking variations one should if possible operate constantly with threats. Here White intends, if allowed, P—K 5-6. Simply 8. Q—Q 2 (2 points) was also good.

8. ...   Kt—Kt 5

*

9. Kt—R 2

2 points. Deduct 5 points for 9. O—O—O?, Kt × P. Instead White exchanges off the annoying knight outpost.

9. ...   Q Kt—B 3

*

10. Kt × Kt

2 points. There is no need, of course, to exchange the useful B at K 2.

10. ...   Kt × Kt

*

11. P—B 3

1 point.

11. ...   Kt—B 3

*

12. O—O—O

2 points. In this position everything favours Q-side castling—an advantage in development, control of the centre, and Black's weakened K-side.

12. ...   Q—R 4

*

13. P—K 5

3 points. White can already break through, since Black cannot capture twice on K 5 owing to mate, while if 13. ... P × P; 14. P × P, Kt—Q 2; 15. P—K 6.

13. ...   Kt—Q 4

77

*

14. Kt × Kt

1 point. White continues energetically without allowing the break-up of his own queen's wing by ... Kt × Kt ch.

14. ...   Q × Kt

*

15. Q—R 3

6 points. The most difficult move of the game—the queen aims at Q 6, K 7, and Q R 7, and so keeps the black king in the centre. 15. P—Q B 4 and 15. P × P (2 points each) maintain the advantage though much less clearly, but deduct 2 points for 15. K—Kt 1, P × P; 16. Q—R 3, P—B 3; when Black escapes.

15. ...   Q—K 3

*

16. P—Q 5

6 points. Another beautiful move; White intends the fine variation 16. ... Q × K P; 17. P—K B 4, Q × B(K 7); 18. K R —K 1, Q × P; 19. B × K P, and wins. 2 points only for 16. P × P, 16. P—K B 4, and 16. K R—K 1, which are not nearly so clear.

16. ...   P × Q P

*

17. P × P

2 points.

17. ...   Q × P

*

18. R × P

6 points. For if 18. ... Q × R; 19. Q × P mate, or 18. ... Q × Q;

19. B—Kt 5 ch, B—Q 2 (19. ... K—B 1; 20. R—Q 8 mate); 20. B × B ch, winning a piece.

18. ...   Q—B 2

*

19. B—Kt 5 ch

4 points for this and 3 points for the pretty 19. R—Q 7 (19. ... B × R; 20. Q × P mate, or 19. ... Q × R; 20. B—Kt 5, Q × B?; 21. Q × P mate), which would win the queen but prolong the game somewhat.

19. ...   K—B 1

*

20. Q—B 5

4 points. This is crushing; if 20. ... Q × Q; 21. R—Q 8 mate.

20. ...   Q—R 4

*

21. B—R 4

5 points. Again better than 21. B—Q 3 (2 points) when Black just avoids mate by 21. ... P—Kt 4; 22. Q × P, Q × Q; 23. R— Q 8 ch, Q—K 1. Now, however, this variation would end up 24. R × Q mate.

21. ...   B × P ch

*

22. K × B

1 point.

22. ...   Q × B

*

23. R—Q 8 ch

1 point.

*

23. ...   K—Kt 2

78

*

24. Q—K 5 ch

1 point.

Black resigns.

It is mate next move.

Summary: A plus in development as great as White's in this game normally makes all kinds of combinative opportunities possible. If you missed some of these chances (White's 13th, 16th, 18th, 19th and 20th) it means your tactical imagination needs sharpening up. Practise, if you can, by looking at the positions in one of the several excellent books on combinations, such as du Mont's 'The Basis of Combination in Chess', or Reinfeld's '1001 Chess Combinations', If you have few opportunities for reading, try in your own games to practise looking briefly round the board each move for combination chances based upon your opponent's king's position or any unguarded pieces he may have.

Game No. 26

In this game you have Black. Your partner is Stojan Puc, of Yugoslavia. Your opponent is Wolfgang Uhlmann of East Germany. The game was played in the international tournament in Krynica, Poland, 1956.
The first moves are 1. P—Q 4, Kt—K B 3; 2. P—Q B 4, P—K 3; 3. Kt—Q B 3, B—Kt 5; 4. P—K 3, P—B 3; 5. B—Q 3, P—Q 3; 6. Kt—K 2, P—K 4; 7. O—O, O—O; 8. P—Q R 3, B—R 4; 9. Q—B 2, R—K 1; 10. P—Q Kt 4, B—B 2; 11. B—Kt 2, Q Kt—Q 2; 12. Kt—Kt 3.

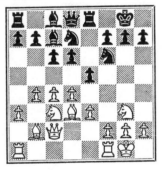

*
12. ...   P—K Kt 3

1 point. Black's previous moves have already foreshadowed a strategy of slow manœuvring in which Black aims to have his pieces actively played however White chooses to open up the position. 12. ... Kt—B 1 (1 point) could also be played here since 13. Kt—B 5, P—K Kt 3; 14. Kt —R 6 ch, K—Kt 2; is not yet a threat.

13. Q R—K 1

*
13. ...   Q—K 2

2 points. This was the intention of his previous move; but 13. ... Kt—B 1 (2 points) is also well playable.

14. R—K 2

*
14. ...   P—K R 4

2 points. The centre is virtually blocked and so it is quite reasonable to begin an action in the wing. 1 point for 14. ... Kt—B 1; which is still quite good, even if not so imaginative as the text.

15. P—B 3

*
15. ...   Kt—B 1
1 point.

16. P—Q 5

White finally tries to make progress in the centre; but now Black's remaining minor pieces can obtain good play.

*
16. ...   P × P

2 points for this, but nothing for 16. ... B—Q 2; when White can control the central outpost at his Q 5 by 17. K Kt—K 4, Kt × Kt; 18. P × Kt!, followed by P—Kt 5.

17. P × P

*
17. ...   B—Q 2

1 point. Nothing for 17. ... B—Kt 3; 18. Kt—R 4.

18. Q—Kt 3

80

*

18. ...   B—Kt 3

1 point for this or 18. ... Q R—B 1.

19. R—B 1

*

19. ...   P—R 5

2 points. This was rather dubious while the white rook was at K B 1 (... Kt × Kt; P × Kt, and White controls the K B file). Now, however, if 20. K Kt—K 4, Kt × Kt; 21. P × Kt, P—B 4; threatening 22. ... P—B 5. (1 point for the sound 19. ... Q R—B 1).

20. Kt—B 1

*

20. ...   Kt—R 4

2 points. The threat is 21. ... Kt—B 5.

21. K—R 1

*

21. ...   Q R—B 1

1 point for this or 21. ... P—B 4; which is equally well playable.

22. Kt—R 4

*

22. ...   B × Kt

2 points. This is better than 22. ... B—Q 1 (22. ... B—B 2; 23. R(K 2)—Q B 2); 23. R × R, B × R; 24. P—Kt 5, with some counterplay. Deduct 2 points for 22. ... P—B 4; 23. Kt × B, P × Kt; 24. R(K 2)—Q B 2, when White can penetrate on the Q B file.

23. Q × B

*

23. ...   Q—Kt 4

2 points for this or 23. ... P—B 4.

24. R—B 4

*

24. ...   P—B 4

1 point.

25. Q—B 2

*

25. ...   R × R

2 points. Black correctly delayed this exchange until White really threatened something on the Q B file.

26. Q × R

*

26. ...   P—B 5

1 point for this move, which, though seemingly powerful, contains a hidden flaw. 3 points for 26. ... R—K 2; after which White is hard put to find a decent defence to the threat of ... R—R 2; ... P—B 5; and a combinative finish beginning with ... Kt—Kt 6 ch.

27. P × P

*

27. ...   Kt × P

1 point. Not 27. ... Q × P? (deduct 1 point); 28. R—K 4.

28. B—B 1

*

28. ...   P—R 6

Deduct 2 points if you chose this move, which loses a piece and should lose the game. 2 points for 28. ... R—K 2; unpinning the K P; which is still best.

29. P—Kt 3

*

29. ...   Q—R 4

1 point.

30. P—Kt 4

*

30. ...   Q—R 5

1 point for this or 30. ... Q—Kt 4.

31. B × Kt

*

31. ...   Q—B 3

1 point.

32. P—K Kt 5

After the correct 32. Kt—Q 2, White should win comfortably with his extra piece.

*

32. ...   Q—B 2

2 points. This unpins the K P.

33. Q—K 4

*

33. ...   P × B

4 points. Black begins a brilliant combination which makes up for his previous mishandling of the attack.

34. Q × R

*

34. ...   Q × P

1 point. White cannot simultaneously defend all the attacked targets as K Kt 5, K B 3, and Q 3.

35. B—B 4

*

35. ...   Q × B

1 point.

36. Q—K 4

*

36. ...   Q—Kt 4

3 points. Another calm *coup de repos.* 37. ... Q × K Kt P is again the threat.

37. P—R 4

Or 37. Q—K 7, B—K 6.

*

37. ...   Q × K Kt P

1 point.

38. Kt—K 3

*

38. ...   B × Kt

1 point.

39. Q—Kt 1

*

39. ...   P—Q 4

2 points. With a material advantage, Black can decide matters by the simplest means.

40. Q—K B 1

*

40. ...   P—Q 5

1 point.

41. R—K 1.

*

41. ...   Q—Kt 7 ch

1 point.

42. Q × Q

*

42. ...   P × Q ch

1 point.

43. K × P

*

43. ...   P—Q 6

1 point.

White resigns, for he is helpless against ... P—Q 7, followed by the knight's arrival at Q B 6.

Summary: The closed centre which occurred in the early middle game enabled Black to carry out long-winded manœuvres, including a complicated king's side attack (moves 19 and 20) which would have been impossible had White been able to hit back in the centre. The later stages of the game, with the mistakes on both sides, illustrate two points where the ordinary club player all too frequently errs; first, Black's blunder on move 28 would surely not have been made had he taken a minute or two to look round the board for tactical drawbacks to his move; second, the violent swing-over on moves 32 and 33 shows once more that a game is never lost until it is won. Bad positions can still contain counterchances which the player, just because he is downhearted at being in difficulties, never looks for properly and so does not notice. Black's final combination seems complicated, but if you failed to collect many marks in this phase of the game, play over these last few moves and see how easy the idea is once you visualize the possible mates on the long white diagonal and at K Kt 8!

Game No. 27

IN this game you have Black. Your partner is M. Tal of Riga, one of the best young attacking players in the world. Your opponent is Szukszta of Poland. The game was played at Uppsala, Sweden, in 1956.

The first moves are 1. P—Q 4, Kt—K B 3; 2. P—Q B 4, P—K Kt 3; 3. Kt—Q B 3, B—Kt 2; 4. P—K 4, P—Q 3; 5. P—B 3, O—O; 6. B—K 3, P—K 4; 7. K Kt—K 2, P—B 3; 8. Q—Kt 3.

*

8. ...   P × P

5 points. Black must try to break open the centre before White has an opportunity to castle. If instead 8 ... Q Kt—Q 2 (1 point); 9. O—O—O, P × P; 10. Kt × P, Kt—B 4; 11. Q—R 3, White has serious pressure on the Q file. Deduct 2 points for 8. ... Q—Kt 3?; 9. Q × Q, P × Q; 10. P × P, winning a pawn. If 8. ... R—K 1 (1 point); 9. O—O—O again gives White opportunities on the Q file.

9. Kt × P

*

9. ...   P—Q 4

6 points. This pawn sacrifice is well justified by the exposure of White's Q B on the open K file. Again, 9. ... R—K 1; and 9. ... Q Kt—Q 2 (1 point each) would be answered by 10. O—O—O.

10. B P × P

*

10. ...   P × P

1 point.

11. P × P

*

11. ...   Kt—B 3

3 points. Black begins an imaginative and brilliant sacrificial combination. However, an inversion of moves with 11. ... R—K 1 (7 points) leads to the same position on move 14 by a better method. If White now replies 12. Kt × Kt, P × Kt; 13. P × P, R—K 1; 14. K—B 2, R × B!; 15. K × R, B—R 3 ch!; 16. P—B 4, Q—K 2 ch; 17. K—B 2 (17. K—Q 3, B—B 4 ch with an overwhelming attack), Kt—Kt 5 ch; and wins.

12. P × Kt

*

12. ...   R—K 1

2 points.

13. K—B 2

Falling into the trap. White could have refuted his opponent's incorrect order of moves by 13. O—O—O!

*

13. ...   R × B

4 points. Now everything clicks. Here, if 14. K × R, B—R 3 ch; 15. P—B 4, Kt—Kt 5 ch; 16. K—K 4, Kt—B 7 ch; 17. K—K 3, B × P ch; 18. K × B, Q × Kt ch; 19. K—B 3, B—Kt 5 ch; 20. K—Kt 3, Q—K 6 ch; 21. K—R 4, P—Kt 4 mate.

14. R—Q 1

Seemingly refuting the whole attack, since both 15. K × R and 15. P × P are threatened.

*

14. ...   Kt—Kt 5 ch

6 points.

15. P × Kt

*

15. ...   B × Kt

1 point.

16. R × B

*

16. ...   Q × R

1 point.

17. Q—Q 5

*

17. ...   R—K 7 db. ch.

7 points. Black must have visualized this beautiful finish before embarking on his whole combination.

18. K × R

*

18. ...   B × P ch

2 points.

19. K—K 1

*

19. ...   R—K 1 ch

3 points.

20. B—K 2

*

20. ...   R × B ch

5 points.

White resigns.

This little masterpiece illustrates above all the value of open files and diagonals. The cross attacks from Black's bishops and major pieces more than outweighed his material deficit. This game is made the more astonishing by the fact that it was played as a lightning encounter with clocks, each player having five minutes for all his moves. Black actually made every move practically instantaneously!

Summary: Black's series of brilliant combinations is based on two factors: the uncastled state of White's king and the insecure situation of his minor pieces in the centre. If you missed some of the combinative moves, go back over the game and, as you reach each critical position, try to visualize in advance the mating and material winning variations which occur.

Game No. 28

In this game you have Black. Your consultation partner is the Hungarian player Kapu. Your opponent is Enej. The game was played in Budapest, 1953.
The first moves are 1. P—K 4, P—Q B 4; 2. Kt—K B 3, Kt—Q B 3; 3. P—Q 4, P × P; 4. Kt × P, Q—B 2; 5. Kt—Q B 3, P—K 3; 6. P—K Kt 3, P—Q R 3; 7. B—Kt 2, Kt—B 3; 8. Kt(Q 4)—K 2, B—K 2; 9. O—O, P—K R 4!; 10. B—Kt 5, P—Kt 4; 11. P—Q R 4, P—Kt 5; 12. Kt—Kt 1, P—R 4; 13. Kt—Q 2.

*

13. ...   B—R 3

2 points. The type of attack which Black is undertaking here—an attack on both wings while keeping the king in the centre, is comparatively rare and normally hazardous. Its justification in this position lies in two factors: firstly, the passive position of the white minor pieces (particularly the knights) and the absence of central strongpoints for White to occupy; this is partly the result of the second factor, Black's majority of

pawns in the centre and the hedge-hog protection which they give in the surrounds of Black's king. It is clear that even at this stage Black's pawn advances on either wing make it impossible for him to castle on either side, so aggression must be the keynote of his play. White must be kept so fully occupied that he cannot prepare an attack himself.

14. Kt—Kt 3
*
14. ...   P—R 5

3 points. Well calculated, for if 15. B × P, R × B!; 16. P × R, Kt—Kt 5; 17. P—K B 4, Kt—K 6; regaining the exchange, while if 15. P × P, Kt—Kt 5; 16. B—B4, B × Kt; 17. B × Q, B × Q; 18. K R × B, R × P; with good counter-chances.

15. B—B 4
*
15. ...   Kt—K 4

2 points. This is clearly superior to 15. ... Q—Kt 2; 16. B—Q 6, or 15. ... P—K 4; 16. B—Kt 5, and White can aim his knights at Q 5 and K B 5, or 15. ... P—Q 3; 16. P—K 5.

16. R—K 1
*
16. ...   P × P
1 point.
17. R P × P
*
17. ...   Kt—R 4
1 point. This at once eliminates the pin and continues the attack.

18. B—Q B 1

86

*

18. ...   Kt—Kt 5

2 points. Black is already looking to K B 7, K Kt 6, and K R 7,
the natural focal points for combinations against White's king.
18. ... P—Kt 4 (2 points) is also
a good attacking move.

19. Kt—B 4

*

19. ...   Kt × Kt

1 point. Deduct 3 points for
moves which leave the knight at
K Kt 5 *en prise.*

20. B × Kt

*

20. ...   Kt—K 4

1 point.

21. Kt—Q 4

*

21. ...   P—Kt 4

3 points. An amusing 'echo' of
the 17th move. Again the pin is
relieved and the attack simultaneously strengthened.

22. B—Q B 1

*

22. ...   R—Q B 1

2 points. It is not every player
who would realize the need for
such an exact move in the middle
of the attack. White is prevented
from carrying out his plan of
Kt—Kt 5, followed by P—K B 4
and P—K 5.

23. P—Kt 3

*

23. ...   P—B 3

3 points. Black gets ready to
unite his rooks for the decisive
assault. 1 point each for 23. ...
P—Kt 5 and for 23. ... B—B 4;
24. Kt—Kt 5, which are less clear.

24. B—K 3

*

24. ...   K—B 2

1 point.

25. R—Q B 1

*

25. ...   R—R 2

2 points. 1 point for 25. ... R—
R 3.

26. Kt—Kt 5.

At last this move is possible, but
it is too late to be effective.

*

26. ...   Q—Kt 1

2 points. Nothing for retreating
the queen to other squares, since
White could then follow with
Kt—Q 6 ch.

27. Q—K 2.

*

27. ...   R(B 1)—R 1

1 point.

28. K R—Q 1

*

28. ...   B—Kt 2

2 points. Trouble is foreshadowed for White on the long
diagonal. This is more certain than
28. ... P—Kt 5; intending to
sacrifice a pawn with ... Kt—
B 6 ch, since White has the reply
29. B—B 4, and in any case
moving the black knight leaves the
Q P loose.

29. B—R 7

87

*
29. ...   Q—R 1

3 points. 29. ... Q—K B 1 (1 point), en route for K R 3, is good, too.

30. B—Q 4

*
30. ...   R—R 8 ch

5 points for this brilliant combination, which decides the game by force.

31. B × R

*
31. ...   R × B ch

1 point.

32. K × R

*
32. ...   B × P ch

1 point.

33. K—Kt 1

*
33. ...   B—B 6

3 points. This is decisive.

34. Kt—B 7

*
34. ...   Q—R 1

1 point.

35. Q × B

*
35. ...   Kt × Q ch

1 point.

36. K—Kt 2

*
36. ...   P—Kt 5

1 point. Despite the reduced material, the mating attack continues.

37. R—K R 1

*
37. ...   Q—Q B 1

2 points for this or 37. ... Q—Q Kt 1. Black wins at least a piece, for if 38. B—Kt 6, Q—Kt 2; 39. B × P, Kt—R 5 db. ch; or 38. Kt—Kt 5, Q—Kt 2; 39. K—B 1, Kt × B.

38. R—R 7 ch

*
38. ...   K—Kt 3

1 point.

39. R(B 1)—K R 1

*
39. ...   Q × Kt

1 point.

40. R(1)—R 6 ch

*
40. ...   K—B 4

1 point.

White resigns.

Summary: Black's whole play revolved round his plan of breaking through on the K R file. If you obtained a bad score on this game, check your play for the consistency with which you carried out this idea.

Game No. 29

IN this game you have White. Your consultation partner is the author of this book. Your opponent is M. E. Wise. The game was played at Twickenham, 1956.

The first moves are 1. Kt—K B 3, Kt—Q B 3; 2. P—K 4, Kt—B 3; 3. P—K 5, Kt—Q 4; 4. P—Q B 4, Kt—Kt 3; 5. P—Q 4, P—Q 3; 6. P—K 6 !, P × P (6. ... B × P; 7. P—Q 5); 7. B—Q 3, P—K Kt 3.

*

8. Kt—Kt 5

3 points. White's 6. P—K 6 indicated his readiness to play a wild gambit. An attempt to return to quiet positional warfare with 8. B—K 3 (no credit) would give Black excellent central counterplay with 8 ... B—Kt 2; 9. O—O, P—K 4.

8. ...   Kt × Q P

*

9. Kt × R P !

3 points. If 9. ... R × Kt; 10. B × P ch.

9. ...   Kt—B 4

*

10. Kt × B

1 point.

10. ...   R × Kt

*

11. B—Kt 5

3 points. White's immediate target is obviously the weak K Kt P; so he aims to play P—K Kt 4 without permitting the powerful reply ... Kt—R 5. 11. P—K R 4 (1 point) with the same idea, is possible, but in a gambit opening White must develop rapidly.

11. ...   B—Q 2

*

12. P—K Kt 4

1 point.

12. ...   B—B 3

*

13. R—Kt 1

1 point for this or the equally good 13. R—B 1.

13. ...   Kt—Kt 2

*

14. B × P ch

1 point.

14. ...   K—Q 2

*

15. Kt—Q 2

2 points. Again clearly best, since the Q B P must be held and neither 15. Q—Q 4, P—K 4; nor 15. P—B 5, Kt—Q 4; are convincing.

15. ...   R—K Kt 1

*

16. P—K R 4

3 points. This safeguards the bishops in their curiously strong position on the K Kt file and at the same time frees White's Q for action at K 2 or Q B 2, according to choice. Positively, the advanced K R P can soon become a real menace to Black.

16. ...   Kt—K 1

*

17. Q—B 2

1 point. As indicated above, 17. P—R 5 (3 points) is more elastic, since it would already threaten 18. Q—K 2 and 19. B—B 7.

17. ...   Kt—B 3

*

18. O—O—O

2 points.

18. ...   Q—K B 1

*

19. P—B 4

2 points for this, 19. Q R—K 1, or 19. P—R 5.

19. ...   P—R 4

*

20. Q R—K 1

2 points for this or 20. P—R 5. Now Black's K P is a target.

20. ...   P—R 5

*

21. P—R 5

3 points. This threatens 22. R × P!, K × R; 23. Q—B 5 mate. Deduct 2 points for the immediate 21. R × P, R × B!

21. ...   R—R 4

Preventing the combination and threatening counter-combinations based on the *vis-à-vis* of White's king and queen.

*

22. K—Kt 1

1 point.

22. ...   R—Q B 4

*

23. B—R 4

5 points for this, which refutes Black's last move, although he does not realize it and continues gaily with

23. ...   B—Q 4

*

24. B—B 2

1 point.

24. ...   Kt × B P

For if 24. ... R—B 3; 25. B × Kt, P × B; 26. Q × P.

*

25. B × R

1 point.

25. ...   Kt × Kt ch

*

26. Q × Kt

1 point.

26. ...   P × B

*

27. P—Kt 5

2 points.

27. ...   Kt—K 1

*

28. P—B 5

2 points. A complete breakthrough.

28. ...   Kt—Q 3

*
29. R(Kt 1)—B 1

2 points. Black still cannot capture the K B P.

29. ...   Q—R 1

*
30. B—B 7

3 points. Black must shed further material.

30. ...   R—K B 1

*
31. P × P ch

1 point for this or 31. B × P ch.

31. ...   K—B 3

*
32. P—Kt 6

1 point. This game is now quickly turning into a massacre. The remaining moves were 32. ...

P—R 6; 33. P—Kt 3, P—B 5;
34. R—K 5, B—K 5 ch; 35. R ×
B, Kt × R; 36. Q—Q 7 ch, K—
Kt 3; 37. Q—Q 4 ch, P—B 4;
38. Q × Kt, P × P; 39. R—B 3,
P × P ch; 40. K × P, R—Q 1;
41. R—Kt 3 ch, K—B 2; 42. Q ×
P ch, Q × Q; 43. R × Q ch, K ×
R; 44. P--Kt 7, Resigns.

Summary: This game contains a series of small tactical points, and if you did not obtain a good score, it means that you should be more on the look-out for snap combinations in your own games. It is also useful practice to work out positions where there is a sacrificial finish—I give two of these each week in my daily column in the *Evening Standard.*

Game No. 30

IN this game you have Black. Your consultation partner is Mikhail Tal, winner of the 1957 Russian Championship, in which he played the present game against V. Gurgenidse. The first moves are 1. P—Q 4, Kt—K B 3; 2. P—Q B 4, P—B 4; 3. P—Q 5, P—K 3; 4. Kt—Q B 3, P × P; 5. P × P, P—Q 3; 6. Kt—B 3, P—K Kt 3; 7. P—K 4, B—Kt 2; 8. B—K 2, O—O; 9. O—O, R—K 1; 10. Kt—Q 2.

*

10. ...   Kt—R 3

2 points. Black plans to combine the action of his K B on the long black diagonal with an advance of his queen's side pawns. For this purpose the Q Kt is best placed on Q B 2. Less good is 10. ... Q Kt—Q 2 (1 point), since the knight can always be driven away from the strongpoint at K 4 by White's P—K B 4.

11. R—K 1

*

11. ...   Kt—B 2

1 point.

12. P—Q R 4

*

12. ...   P—Kt 3

2 points. This or 12. ... R—Kt 1 (2 points) are a necessary preparation for ... P—Q R 3 and ... P—Q Kt 4; since the immediate 12. ... P—Q R 3 (no credit) is strongly answered by 13. P—R 5, followed in some variations by Kt—R 4—Kt 6.

13. Q—B 2

*

13. ...   Kt—Kt 5

4 points. Another characteristic of the aggressive opening which Black has adopted is that he can often attack on both wings. Objectively, the move is no stronger than 13. ... P—Q R 3 or 13. ... R—Kt 1 (3 points each); but it contains a profound and beautiful trap, into which White falls.

14. P—R 3

*

14. ...   Kt × B P

6 points. Black begins a brilliant combinative sequence with this fine move.

15. K × Kt

*

15. ...   Q—R 5 ch

2 points for this or B—Q 5 ch.

16. K—B 1

*

16. ...   B—Q 5

1 point.

17. Kt—Q 1

*
17. ...   Q × R P

6 points. This was the real idea of the combination. Of course, if 18. P × Q, B × P mate; and now White's king can never find a safe haven. Deduct 2 points for 17. ... B × R P?; which would actually lose after 18. Kt—K B 3.

18. B—B 3
*
18. ...   Q—R 7

3 points. Now the threat is 19. ... Kt × P; 20. P × Kt?, Q—Kt 8 mate.

19. Kt—K 3
*
19. ...   P—B 4

4 points. This is clearer than 19. ... B—R 3 ch; 20. Kt(Q 2)—B 4, P—B 4; 21. P × P. Black opens up all the lines for his attack.

20. Kt(Q 2)—B 4
*
20. ...   P × P
1 point.
21. B × P
*
21. ...   B—R 3

2 points. Now this move results in the strangulation of all White's pieces.

22. B—B 3
*
22. ...   R—K 4

3 points. This simultaneously puts pressure on the Q P and prepares to double rooks.

23. R—R 3

*
23. ...   Q R—K 1
1 point.
24. B—Q 2
*
24. ...   Kt × P

5 points. Another variation on the mating theme already introduced on move 18. If 25. B × Kt ch, R × B; 26. Kt × R?, Q—Kt 8 mate.

25. B × Kt ch
*
25. ...   R × B
1 point.
26. K—K 2
*
26. ...   B × Kt(K 6)

4 points. This is decisive, for if 27. B × B, Q × P is mate.

27. R × B
*
27. ...   B × Kt ch

2 points.

White resigns, for if 28. Q × B, Q × P ch; and mate next move.

Summary: The beautiful 'flowing' impression produced by this attack can really be analysed into Black's awareness of a series of short tactical combinations. Whether or not you found the initial knight sacrifice is mainly a test of your combinative intuition; but if you did badly on the rest of the game it shows that you are most likely missing numerous tactical chances in your own games.

VII CONSTRICTION TECHNIQUE

Game No. 31

IN this game you have White. Your consultation partner is Salo Flohr. Your opponent is P. Frydman. The game was played at Ujpest, 1934.

The first moves are 1. P—Q 4, Kt—K B 3; 2. Kt—K B 3, P—K 3; 3. P—K 3, P—Q Kt 3; 4. B—Q 3, B—Kt 2; 5. Q Kt—Q 2, P—B 4; 6. O—O, B—K 2; 7. P—B 4, O—O; 8. P—Q Kt 3, P—Q 3; 9. B—Kt 2, Q Kt—Q 2; 10. Q—K 2, Q—B 2; 11. P—K 4, P—K 4; 12. P—Q 5, Kt—R 4; 13. P—Kt 3, P—Kt 3.

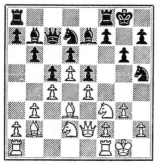

*

14. Kt—K 1

2 points. In completely blocked positions such as this, the correct technique for the player possessing the greater share of the board is to increase this space advantage as much as possible in the hope that, sooner or later, the opponent's lack of manœuvring room

will enable the stronger party to break through, even at the cost of considerable sacrifices. Here White's obvious first objective is to build a strong position on the K B file.

14. ...   Q R—B 1

*

15. Kt—Kt 2

1 point for this or 15. P—B 4.

15. ...   P—B 3

*

16. Q R—K 1

1 point for this or P—B 4.

16. ...   R—B 2

*

17. P—B 4

1 point.

17. ...   Kt—Kt 2

*

18. P—B 5

2 points. White could also try the effect of tripling his heavy pieces on the K B file with R—B 3 (2 points), Q R—K B 1, R(B 1)—B 2, and Q—B 1, but Black's last three moves have shown that he is ready to meet this by ... Q R—K B 1; ... Q—Q 1; and ... Q—K 1; when everything is held.

18. ...   R—Q 1

*

19. B—B 1

1 point for this, 19. P—K R 4, 19. R—B 3, or 19. R—B 2. White concentrates everything on the K side and prepares for a long and patient siege. There is no need to look for meaning in Black's moves, however, as he can do absolutely nothing until it is clear exactly what plan White is going to adopt.

19. ...   Kt—K 1

*

20. R—B 2

1 point for this, 20. R—B 3, or 20. P—K R 4.

20. ...   B—K B 1

*

21. Kt—B 1

1 point for this or 21. P—K R 4.

21. ...   P—K Kt 4

*

22. P—K R 4

1 point.

22. ...   P—K R 3

*

23. Kt(Kt 2)—K 3

3 points. The second stage of the game is reached. It is now clear that White's break through will come, if anywhere, on the K R file, and White accordingly prepares to triple his heavy pieces on this file before opening it. Note that this is invariably the strategy in such positions; to exchange pawns now (deduct 2 points) or at any time before White has tripled would give Black access to extra squares on the K R file and thus enable him to contest it with his own heavy pieces.

23. ...   R—R 2

*

24. R—R 2

1 point.

24. ...   B—Kt 2

*

25. Q—Q 1

4 points. Obscure? To explain the reason for this would also give away the next few moves as well!

25. ...   Kt—B 1

*

26. B—K 2

2 points.

26. ...   B—B 1

*

27. Kt—Q 2

1 point.

27. ...   Q—K 2

*

28. K—Kt 2

1 point.

28. ...   Kt—B 2

*

29. B—R 5

2 points. This explains White's 25th and 26th moves. By establishing the B at K Kt 6 he makes it impossible for Black to put up any proper opposition to the invasion on the K R file except by exchanging his own white-squared, useful, bishop for it. White's 27th and 28th moves were part of the general preparation for occupying the K R file. They could equally have come earlier, so take full credit if you chose either of these moves on White's 25th and 26th.

29. ...   B—Q 2

*
30. B—Kt 6
1 point.
30. ...   R—K R 1
*
31. R(K 1)—R 1
2 points.
31. ...   B—K 1
*
32. B × B
1 point.
32. ...   Kt × B
*
33. Kt—B 3
1 point.
33. ...   R—R 2
*
34. R—R 3
3 points, and 1 point if you chose this on the previous move.
34. ...   R—Q 2
*
35 R(1)—R 2
1 point.
35. ...   Q—Q 1
*
36. Q—R 1
1 point.
36. ...   B—R 1
*
37. P × P
2 points.
37. ...   R P × P
*
38. Kt—Kt 4
1 point. Note how White's impeccable strategy has not only opened the K R file in the most favourable circumstances possible, but has also placed his minor pieces on the squares where they have the maximum opportunity for joining the attack. Deduct 3 points if you chose 37. Kt—Kt 4??, last move, for Black simply replies 37. ... P—K R 4; and ... P—Kt 5.

38. ...   R × R
*
39. R × R
1 point.
39. ...   Kt—R 2
*
40. R—R 6
1 point. The logical consequence of the undisputed possession of the open file is this penetration of Black's defences.
40. ...   P—R 3
*
41. Q—R 5
2 points.
41. ...   P—Kt 4
*
42. B × P
4 points. A typical sacrifice in such positions—the crammed position of Black's minor pieces prevents him from organizing a reasonable resistance.
42. ...   P × B
*
43. Kt × Kt P
1 point.
43. ...   Kt—Kt 2

*

44. R—Kt 6

2 points.

44. ...   Kt × Kt

*

45. R × Kt(Kt 5)

1 point.

Black resigns, for he has no defence against the threat of 46. P—B 6 and 47. P—B 7 ch (47. ... R × P; 48. Kt—R 6 ch).

Summary: Like game No. 18 (Persitz-Galula) this game illustrates the treatment of closed positions where the opponent is permanently cramped. If you chose moves which opened up the game too quickly, take note of how methodically Flohr makes his preparations, and does not begin his final sacrificial attack until his pieces are close to the scene of action and Black's king's position is already weakened by the exchange of the white-squared bishops.

VIII THE ENDING

Game No. 32

IN this ending you have Black. Your consultation partner is world championship candidate Paul Keres. Your opponent is the veteran British master E. G. Sergeant. The game was played at Margate, 1939.

The first part of the game went as follows: 1. P—K 4, P—K 4; 2. Kt—K B 3, Kt—Q B 3; 3. B—Kt 5, P—Q R 3; 4. B—R 4, Kt—B 3; 5. O—O, P—Q 3; 6. R—K 1, B—Q 2; 7. P—B 3, B—K 2; 8. P—Q 4, O—O; 9. Q Kt—Q 2, R—K 1; 10. P—K R 3 (passive; better is 10. B—Kt 3), B—K B 1; 11. B—B 2, P—K Kt 3; 12. Kt—B 1, B—Kt 2; 13. Kt—Kt 3, Q—K 2; 14. B—K 3, Q R—Q 1; 15. P—Q 5, Kt—Kt 1; 16. Q—Q 2, Q R—B 1; 17. K R—Q 1, Q—B 1; 18. Kt—R 2, K—R 1; 19. R—K B 1, B—Kt 4; 20. B—Q 3, B × B; 21. Q × B, Kt—Kt 1; 22. P—K B 4? (allowing Black to use his K 4 as a focal point for manœuvring), P × P; 23. B × P, Kt—Q 2; 24. Kt—B 3, P—R 3; 25. Q R—K 1, Q—K 2; 26. B—K 3, Kt—K 4; 27. Kt × Kt, B × Kt; 28. B—Q 4, R—B 1; 29. Q—B 3, Q R—K 1; 30. Kt—K 2, K—Kt 2; 31. B × B ch, Q × B; 32. Kt—B 4, Kt—B 3; 33. Kt—Q 3, Q—Kt 4; 34. K—R 2, Kt—Q 2; 35. P—K Kt 3, Kt—K 4; 36. Kt × Kt, R × Kt; 37. Q—B 4, Q—K 2; 38. P—K Kt 4, P—K R 4; 39. P—B 4, Q—R 5; 40. R—K 3, P × P; 41. Q × P, R—K R 1; 42. R(3)—K B 3, R—K 2; 43. K—Kt 2, R—R 4; 44. Q × Q, R × Q; 45. R—B 4, R × R; 46. R × R.

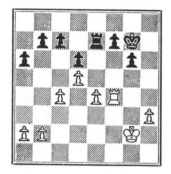

*

46. ... P—K Kt 4

3 points. This endgame is favourable to Black because White has several weaknesses—his K 5 square, his K P, and his K R P. However, the ending presents many technical difficulties since Black's king and rook are bound to look after his own K B P, and the natural way to win, by penetrating with the black king through the black squares, is not available here; the black king cannot reach the square K 4 owing to the white rook's position.

98

So as a first step to strengthening his position Black aims to manœuvre his rook to a square where it attacks both the weak white pawns.

47. R—Kt 4

*

47. ...   K—Kt 3!

3 points. Clearly calculated, for White cannot eliminate his weak K R P by 48. P—K R 4, K—R 4; 49. R × P ch (49 K—Kt 3, R—K 4!, or 49. K—R 3, P × P; 50. R × P ch, K—Kt 4; followed by ... K—B 3—K 4), K × P; 50. R—Kt 7, R × P; 51. R × P, R × P.

48. K—B 3

*

48. ...   P—K B 3

2 points. Now White can eliminate the K R P, but only at the cost of allowing Black's rook to penetrate: 49. P—K R 4, K—R 4; 50. P × P, P × P (threat 50. ... R—B 2 ch); 51. R—Kt 2, R—B 2 ch; 52. K—K 2, R—B 5; 53. K—K 3, R—B 8. Nothing for 48. ... K—R 4; when Black cannot make further progress, since his rook is tied to the K B P.

49. R—Kt 2

*

49. ...   R—R 2
2 points.

50. K—Kt 3

*

50. ...   R—R 5
2 points. Thus the plan is completed.

51. R—K 2

*

51. ...   R—B 5

2 points. The next stage begins; Black penetrates with his rook.

52. P—Kt 4

*

52. ...   R—B 8
1 point.

53. R—Q B 2

*

53. ...   R—Kt 8

2 points. Naturally he does not allow the counterplay beginning 54. P—B 5.

54. P—Kt 5

*

54. ...   P—R 4

1 point. Black is only too glad to see the pawn position definitely fixed. Static weaknesses are the easiest to attack, and here not one of White's chain of pawns has a hope of becoming mobile. Deduct 3 points for the blunder 54. ... P × P; 55. P × P, R × P; 56. R × P, when White draws easily.

55. K—Kt 4

*

55. ...   P—Kt 3

1 point. Now the pawn chain is completely immobile.

56. K—Kt 3

*

56. ...   R—Q 8

2 points. It is a characteristic of positions where one side has an active against a passive rook that the former can continually make threats, in this case 57. ... R—

Q 6 ch; followed by ... R—K 6 or ... R × R P, winning a pawn.

57. R—B 3

*

57. ...   R—Q 7

2 points.

58. P—R 3

*

58. ...   P—R 5

3 points. Another threat; this time it is ... R—Q Kt 7—Kt 6.

59. P—R 4

*

59. ...   R—K 7

4 points. Here 59. ... R—Kt 7 (2 points) should win, although White has some faint chances by 60. K—Kt 4, R—Kt 6; 61. P—R 5 ch, K—R 3; 62. R—B 2, R × R P; 63. R—B 2, K—Kt 2; 64. P—R 6 ch. The text is much clearer.

60. P × P

*

60. ...   K × P

2 points. Nothing for 60. ... P × P; when there might follow 61. K—B 3, R—K R 7; 62. K—Kt 4, R—Q Kt 7; 63. P—K 5!, P × P; 64. P—B 5!, R × P?; 65. P—Q 6, B P × P; 66. P—B 6.

61. K—B 3

*

61. ...   R—K R 7

2 points.

62. K—K3

Or 62. K—Kt 3, R—Q Kt 7.

*

62. ...   R—R 6 ch

1 point.

63. K—Q 4

*

63. ...   R × R

1 point.

64. K × R

*

64. ...   K—Kt 5

2 points. But not 64. ... K—B 5 (deduct 3 points); 65. K—Q 4, keeping the opposition, and draws!

65. K—Q 4

*

65. ...   K—B 5

1 point.

66. K—Q 3

*

66. ...   K—B 6

1 point.

67. K—Q 4

*

67. ...   K—K 7

2 points.

68. K—B 3

*

68. ...   K—K 6

1 point.

69. K—Kt 4

*

69. ...   K × P

1 point. The weak pawn (created on move 22!) falls at last.

70. K × P

*

70. ...   P—K B 4

1 point.

71. K—Kt 3

*

71. ...   K—Q 6

4 points. Now White's king cannot approach the pawn.

72. P—R 4

*

72. ...   P—B 5

1 point. White resigns. If 73. P—R 5, P—B 6; 74. P—R 6, P—B 7; 75. P—R 7, P—B 8(Q); 76. P—R 8(Q), Q—Kt 8 ch; 77. K—R 3, Q—R 8 ch.

Summary: In rook and pawn endings the most important principle of all is to keep your rook active. Note how in this game Keres utilizes his opponent's need to defend his weakened pawns by penetrating with his rook and thus making White's rook entirely a defensive piece. If you went wrong at Black's 46th, 50th, 52nd, or 54th moves, you are not fully conversant with the principle. There is a good section on rook and pawn endings in Reinfeld's 'Practical Endgame Play', and most anthologies of games include one or more of the great rook and pawn endings of Rubinstein. Study also Game No. 33 (Wade-Czerniak) in this book.

Game No. 33

IN this ending you have White. Your consultation partner is former British champion Bob Wade. Your opponent is Israel champion Miguel Czerniak. The game was played in the 1950 Venice tournament.

The first part of the game went as follows: 1. P—K 4, P—K Kt 3; 2. P—Q 4, B—Kt 2; 3. P—K Kt 3, P—Q 3; 4. B—Kt 2, Kt—K B 3; 5. Kt—K 2, O—O; 6. O—O, P—K 4; 7. P—Q B 3, Kt—B 3; 8. Kt—Q 2, Kt—K R 4; 9. Kt—Q B 4, P—B 4 ?; 10. K P × P, Kt P × P; 11. P × P, P × P; 12. Q × Q, Kt × Q (Black's opening involves lasting pawn weaknesses).

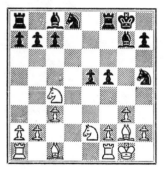

*
13. B—B 3

2 points. This was the idea of the exchange of queens. Now if 13. ... Kt—K B 3; simply 14. Kt × P.

13. ...   B—K 3

*
14. Kt × P

3 points. The well-known 'desperado' combination is here much better than 14. B × Kt, B × Kt; or 14. Kt—K 3, Kt—K B 3; (no credit for either of these) after which Black's minor pieces are, if anything, the better placed.

14. ...   Kt × P

*
15. R P × Kt

1 point. Again this is the only reasonable move, for White cannot continue the 'desperado' sequence owing to the threat to his rook. 15. Kt × Kt would unnecessarily separate the pawns, and there is no reason for disobeying the general rule that pawn captures should be made towards the centre.

15. ...   B × Kt

*
16. Kt—B 4

2 points. Other moves also quite playable here are 16. B—R 6 and 16. B—B 4 (2 points each). The last-mentioned might even seem the most thematic, since the weakness of Black's Q Kt P and the placing of both his K-side pawns on white squares makes Black's Q B potentially a ' bad ' bishop with little attacking scope compared with its white counterpart operating on white squares. However, White judges that this plan of campaign can be tried later on; first he explores the possibility of obtaining the two bishops.

16. ...   B—B 2

102

*

17. R—K 1

2 points. One of the hallmarks which distinguish a master from a strong amateur is the consistency with which the former simplifies the position when his opponent has lasting positional weaknesses. This forced further simplification is the only advantage which the text-move has over 17. R—Q 1 (1 point), since if now 17. ... B—Q 3; 18. Kt—R 5, Kt—K 3; 19. B—R 6, and Black's difficulties increase.

17. ...   R—K 1

*

18. Kt—Q 3

1 point.

18. ...   B—Q 3

*

19. R × R ch

1 point.

19. ...   B × R

*

20. B—B 4

2 points. To return to the previous plan with 20. Kt—B 4 (1 point) would allow Black near-equality by 20. ... B—B 3; 21. Kt—Q 5, K—B 2. So White deprives the Q B P of its defender and at the same time exchanges Black's most active remaining piece.

20. ...   B × B

*

21. Kt × B

2 points. Not 21. P × B, since White must visualize that in the

later ending he may be able to attack the weak K B P by occupying the square in front of it with his king.

21. ...   B—B 3

*

22. Kt—Q 5

1 point. Obtaining the advantage of bishop against knight in an open position, for if 22. ... R—B 1 (to defend the Q B P); 23. Kt—K 7 ch.

22. ...   B × Kt

*

23. B × B ch

1 point.

23. ...   K—B 1

*

24. R—Q 1

3 points. Much stronger than 24. K—Kt 2 or 24. R—K 1 (no credit), since Black's knight is now confined to the back rank for some time to come (24. ... Kt—B 2; 25. B × Kt and 26. R—Q 7 ch). This illustrates a general principle governing the play of the side with the bishop in B v. Kt endings; in an open position, the bishop can be utilized to restrict the knight's activity.

24. ...   P—Q R 4

*

25. R—Q 4

4 points. Another very constructive move. It is generally known that the ideal situation to aim for in rook and pawn endings is to penetrate with the rook to the seventh rank, among the enemy

103

pawns, but there is less awareness of the strength of combining
vertical and horizontal rook man-
oeuvres. Now White wins the
K B P by force, e.g. 25.... R—R 3;
26. R—K B 4, R—K B 3; 27. B—
K 4, or 25. ... K—K 2; 26. R—
K B 4, K—B 3; 27. B—K 4.

25. ...   P—B 3

*

26. B—Kt 3

2 points. The B naturally stays
on the diagonal where it restricts
the Kt, and 26. B—B 4?, P—
Q Kt 4; would cost an important
tempo.

26. ...   P—Q Kt 4

*

27. R—K B 4
1 point.

27. ...   P—R 5

*

28. R × P ch
1 point.

28. ...   K—Kt 2

*

29. B—B 2
1 point.

29. ...   Kt—K 3

*

30. K—B 1

2 points. White is a pawn up and
he must consolidate it against a
possible counter-attack. Bringing
the king to the centre is the
obvious and only way to meet the
threat of ... R—Q 1—Q 7.

30. ...   R—Q 1

*

31. K—K 2
1 point.

31. ...   P—R 3

*

32. B—K 4

2 points. A further phase of
consolidation; Black is again
forced back to passive defence (32.
... P—B 4; 33. B—B 6).

32. ...   R—Q 3

*

33. P—K B 4

2 points. This not only begins
the advance of the passed pawn,
but deprives the knight of the
square K Kt 4.

33. ...   P—Kt 5

*

34. P—R 3

5 points. By fixing the queen's
side White deprives his opponent
of the least counter-chance. Deduct 7 points for 34. P × P??,
Kt—Q 5 ch.

34. ...   P × R P

*

35. P × P
1 point.

35. ...   Kt—B 2

*

36. R—B 5

4 points. Now another pawn is
ripe for execution. Nothing for
36. R—Q R 5, Kt—Kt 4; 37. R ×
P??, Kt × P ch.

36. ...   Kt—Kt 4

*

37. B × P

3 points. Deduct 2 points for 37. R × P?, R × R; 38. B × R, Kt × P ch; 39. K—Q 3, Kt—Kt 8 when Black most likely draws.

37. ...   Kt × R P

*

38. B × P

1 point.

With two pawns up, White's win is now easy. The remaining moves were 38. ... R—K 3 ch; 39. K—Q 2, R—K Kt 3; 40. K—B 1, R—Kt 3; 41. R—B 7 ch, K—B 1; 42. B—Q 1, R—Kt 8 ch; 43. K—

Q 2, Kt—Kt 4; 44. R—Q Kt 7, Kt × P; 45. R × R, Kt × R ch; 46. K—Q 3, K—Kt 2 (if 46. ... Kt—R 6; 47. B—R 4, and the knight remains trapped); 47. B—K 2, Kt—R 6; 48. K—B 3, P—R 4; 49. K—Kt 2, P—R 5; 50. P × P, Resigns.

Summary: Another instance of the value of playing to a plan. White's whole conduct of the ending was based on the fact that, if he could retain his initiative and development advantage, Black's weak pawns must eventually begin to tumble.

Game No. 34

IN this game you have White. Your consultation partner is the author. Your opponent is former British champion R. J. Broadbent. The game was played in London, 1956.

The first part of the game went:
1. P—K 4, P—K 3; 2. P—Q 4, P—Q 4; 3. Kt—Q B 3, Kt—K B 3; 4. P—K 5, K Kt—Q 2; 5. P—B 4, P—Q B 4; 6. P × P, B × P; 7. Kt—B 3, Kt—Q B 3; 8. B—Q 3, P—Q R 3; 9. P—Q R 3, Q—B 2; 10. Q—K 2, Kt—Q 5; 11. Kt × Kt, B × Kt; 12. Kt—Q 1, Kt—B 4; 13. B—K 3, B × B; 14. Q × B, B—Q 2; 15. O—O, R—Q B 1; 16. Kt—B 3, P—K Kt 3; 17. Q R—B 1, Q—Kt 3; 18. R—Kt 1, Kt—R 5; 19. Q × Q, Kt × Q.

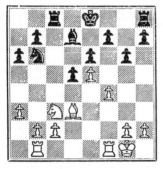

*

20. Kt—K 2

1 point for this or 20. K—B 2. White's advantage here is that his opponent has a bishop hemmed in by its own pawns, a frequent occurrence in the French Defence and Queen's Gambit Declined. Thus baldly stated, the position is still meaningless; but the consequence of so many black pawns being on white squares is that it is quite easy for white's king and knight to obtain good posts on black squares, particularly on the central point Q 4. White's advantage is limited here by the fact that Black has a minor piece which can also operate on black squares; consequently White will try to exchange his opponent's knight against his own relatively inactive bishop; Black, conversely, will try to exchange off his own bishop for either of White's minor pieces.

White has a second advantage in his somewhat greater command of space (centre pawn on the fifth); he will strive to exploit his resulting superior mobility by preparing a breakthrough, the most natural areas for which are on the K B and K R files.

20. ...   Kt—R 5

*

21. Kt—Q 4

1 point for this or 21. K—B 2.

21. ...   K—K 2

*

22. K—B 2

1 point.

22. ...   R—B 2

*

23. K—K 3

1 point. 2 points, however, if you chose P—K Kt 4 here or on the previous two moves. P—

K Kt 4 would soon prepare P—B 5, which Black now delays.

23. ...   P—K R 4

*

24. P—K Kt 3

1 point. White envisaged P—K R 3 and P—K Kt 4. A good alternative was 24. P—B 3 (1 point), preparing to drive away the enemy knight by B—B 2 (as outlined above, Black should not allow his knight to be exchanged). Deduct a point for the positional blunder 24. P—K R 3?, P—R 5; when White can never mobilize his K side (25. K—B 3, R(B 2)—B 1; 26. K—Kt 4, R—R 2; 27. Kt—B 3, R(B 1)—K R 1).

24. ...   R(R 1)—Q B 1

*

25. P—R 3

1 point for this or 25. P—B 3.

25. ...   Kt—B 4

*

26. R—K R 1

1 point. A final preparation for 27. P—K Kt 4, which could also be played immediately (1 point).

26. ...   R—K R 1

*

27. P—K Kt 4

1 point.

27. ...   Kt × B

A positional mistake in time trouble. As outlined in the note to move 20, Black should have avoided this move above all.

28. K × Kt

1 point, but 2 points for 28. P × Kt, which is much better since it gives White two open files instead of one; generally, the side with the greater mobility should strive for open lines.

28. ...   B—Kt 4 ch

*

29. K—K 3

1 point. Deduct 2 points for the positional blunder 29. Kt × B?.

29. ...   B—R 5

*

30. P—B 3

1 point.

30. ...   R(B 2)—B 1

Correct was 30. ... B—Q 2; when it would still be very difficult for White to make progress.

*

31. P—B 5

2 points. This is the only way to win.

31. ...   K P × P

*

32. P × B P

1 point.

32. ...   B—Q 2

*

33. P—B 6 ch

1 point. Nothing for 33. P × P, P × P; when although White has more open lines to work on, he can scarcely win owing to the weakness of his K P.

33. ...   K—Q 1

*
34. Q R—Q 1

2 points. White prepares a re-grouping manœuvre in which he will attack both the Q P and the K B P, the latter by Kt—B3—Kt 5. 1 point only for 34. Kt—B 3 at once, which is less clear (34. ... B—B 4; 35. Q R—Q 1, B—K 5).

34. ...   K—B 2

*
35. Kt—B 3
1 point.

35. ...   B—K 3

*
36. P—K R 4

2 points. This systematic strengthening of the black squares is safer than 36. Kt—Kt 5 (1 point), P—R 5!; followed by ... R—R 4.

36. ...   K—Q 2

*
37. R—Q 4

2 points. 37. Kt—Kt 5 (1 point), R—B 5!; 38. K R—K 1, K R—Q B 1; might still make it hard for White to obtain a winning position. Now if 37. ... R—B 5; 38. R × R, P × R; 39. R—Q 1 ch, K—B 3; 40. Kt—Kt 5, followed by Kt—K 4—Q 6, and Black's totally passive position must crack up.

37. ...   P—Q Kt 4

*
38. P—R 4

2 points. Black's last move left open a welcome new entry route on the Q R file.

38. ...   K—B 3

*
39. R—R 1
1 point.

39. ...   K R—B 1

*
40. P × P ch.
1 point.

40. ...   P × P

*
41. R—Q Kt 4
1 point.

41. ...   K—Kt 3

Black can just avoid losing a pawn for the moment.

*
42. Kt—Q 4
1 point.

42. ...   B—Q 2

*
43. R—Kt 3

2 points. There is nothing more to be done by direct attack on the Q Kt P (since Black has ... R—B 4; available), and so White takes possession of the only open file.

43. ...   R—Q R 1

*
44. R(3)—R 3
1 point. 44. R × R (1 point) is equally good, for if 44. ... R × R; 45. R—R 3, R × R; 46. P × R, K—B 4?; 47. P—K 6!

44. ...   R × R

*
45. R × R
1 point.

45. ...   R—B 1

108

*
46. K—B 4

2 points. Now White can invade on the opposite wing—note how White's hegemony of the black squares gives him easy entry routes.

46. ...   R—K 1

*
47. Kt—B 3

2 points. The threat is 48. K—Kt 5, or if 47. ... B—Kt 5; 48. Kt—Kt 5.

47. ...   R—Q B 1

*
48. K—Kt 5

1 point.

48. ...   R—K 1

*
49. K—R 6

3 points; this logical move needs accurate calculation.

49. ...   B—Kt 5

*
50. Kt—Q 4

2 points; nothing for 50. Kt—Kt 5, R × P; 51. Kt × P, R—B 4!

50. ...   R × P

*
51. R—R 7

5 points. The main variation which White had to work out continues 51. ... K × R; 52. Kt—B 6 ch, K—Kt 3; 53. Kt × R, B—K 3; 54. K—Kt 7, K—B 2 (54. ... P—Kt 4; 55. P × P, P—R 5; 56. Kt—B 3, followed by P—Kt 6); 55. Kt × B P, B × Kt; 56. K × B, P—Kt 4; 57. K—Kt 7 and wins.

51. ...   R—K 5?

This loses immediately.

*
52. R × P

1 point.

52. ...   B—Q 8

*
53. R—K 7

1 point.

Black resigns.

Summary: If you obtained a bad score on this ending, it was probably because you did not sufficiently appreciate the importance of keeping Black's 'bad' bishop restricted. Study some examples of this type of ending in Fine's 'Basic Chess Endings', or Reinfeld's 'Practical Endgame Play'.

Game No. 35

In this ending you have Black. Your consultation partner is the young Yugoslav Andrija Fuderer, who is equally as brilliant at chemistry and piano-playing as at the chessboard. Your opponent is Dr. Heinz Lehmann of West Germany, a frequent competitor in English tournaments. The game was played at Munich, 1954.

The first part of the game went as follows: 1. P—K 4, P—Q B 4; 2. Kt—K B 3, P—Q 3; 3. P—B 3, Kt—K B 3; 4. B—Q 3, Kt—B 3; 5. B—B 2, B—Kt 5; 6. P—K R 3, B × Kt; 7. Q × B, P—K Kt 3; 8. P—Q 3, B—Kt 2; 9. O—O, O—O; 10. Kt—Q 2, P—Q Kt 4; 11. Q—K 2, Kt—Q 2; 12. Kt—B 3, R—B 1; 13. B—K 3, P—Kt 5; 14. P × P, Kt × P; 15. B—Kt 3, Q—Kt 3; 16. Q R—Q 1, Kt—Q B 3; 17. Q—Q 2, R—Kt 1; 18. B—R 6, Kt(Q 2)—K 4; 19. Kt × Kt, B × B; 20. Q × B, P × Kt; 21. B—Q 5, Kt—Q 5; 22. R—Q 2, Q—R 4; 23. P—B 3, R—Kt 3; 24. R(Q 2)—K B 2, R—K B 3; 25. Q—Kt 5, Q—B 2; 26. Q—Q 2, R—B 1; 27. K—R 1, K—Kt 2; 28. R—B 1, R—Kt 3; 29. Q—R 5, P—Kt 4; 30. P—Q R 3, P—K 3; 31. B—R 2, K—B 3; 32. P—Q Kt 4, R—B 3; 33. Q × Q, R(B 1) × Q; 34. B—B 4, P × P; 35. P × P, R—Kt 3; 36. R—Kt 2, R(B 2)—Kt 2; 37. R—R 1, R × P; 38. R × R, R × R; 39. R × P.

*

39. ...   R—Kt 8 ch

4 points. Black's positional advantage in this ending is a typical instance of a knight's superiority over a bishop hemmed in by its own pawns. All White's pawns are on white squares, and his bishop's only hope of activity is to join with the rook in an operation against Black's K B P. In terms of actual moves, Black can aim at an obvious winning situation. If he can transfer his knight to K B 5, and his rook to the seventh, White will be obliged (since his bishop cannot get back inside his pawn-chain) to defend his K Kt P with his rook. Then the black king simply walks round to K Kt 6. Black therefore begins by tying down his opponent's king to the K Kt P. This is still more effective if a pin operates as well, so only 2 points for the immediate 39. ... R—Kt 7.

40. K—R 2

*

40. ...   R—Kt 7

2 points.

41. K—R 1

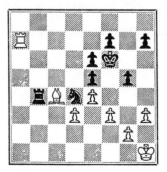

110

*

41. ...   P—R 4

3 points. 1 point for 41. ... Kt—
K 7; but by advancing the R P to
R 5, White is deprived of any faint
chances with P—K R 4.

42. R—R 2

Otherwise Black simply carries
out his plan outlined in the note
to move 39.

*

42. ...   R × R

3 points. 42. ... R—Kt 8 ch
(take no credit) would probably
not lead to a win, since White's
K Kt 2 can then be adequately
defended.

43. B ×R

*

43. ...   Kt—K 7

6 points. Again the only correct
move, for upon 43. ... K—K 2 or
43. ... P—R 5 (no credit); 44. K—
Kt 1 enables White's king to join
in the game.

44. B—B 4

*

44. ...   P—R 5

3 points.

45. K—R 2

*

45. ...   Kt—B 5

No credit for this move, after
which White could have obtained
good drawing chances by the
obvious 46. P—Kt 3, but 4 points
for 45. ... K—K 2, intending to
bring the king to K 6, and, if
necessary, advance the K B P to

K B 5 before launching the final
attack on the Q P.

46. K—Kt 1?

*

46. ...   K—K 2

3 points. Now everything runs
smoothly again.

47. B—Kt 5

*

47. ...   K—Q 3

1 point.

48. B—K 8

*

48. ...   P—B 3

2 points. 1 point for 48. ... P—
B 4; which is no longer essential.

49. B—Kt 5

*

49. ...   K—B 4

1 point.

50. B—B 4

*

50. ...   K—Q 5

1 point.

51. K—B 1

*

51. ...   K—B 6

6 points for this, but nothing for
51. ... Kt × Q P; 52. B × P,
when White draws, nor for 51. ...
K—K 6; 52. K—Kt 1, K—Q 7;
53. K—B 1! and Black is not
making progress.

52. K Kt 1

If K—B 2, Kt × Q P is *check*.

111

*

52. ...   K—B 7

4 points. No credit for anything else.

53. K—R 2

Virtually resignation, but if 53. K—B 2, Kt × Q P ch; or 53. K—B 1, K—Q 7!; 54. K—Kt 1, K—K 8!; 55. K—R 2, K—B 7.

*

53. ...   K—Q 7

4 points.

54. P—Kt 3

*

54. ...   Kt × Q P

2 points. But again not 54. ... P × P ch; 55. K × P, and draws.

55. B × P

*

55. ...   K—K 6

2 points.

56. P × P

If 56. K—Kt 2, Kt—K 8 ch; or 56. B—Kt 4, Kt—K 8; and in either case Black wins.

*

56. ...   P × P

1 point.

White resigns.

Summary: Like Game No. 34, this ending illustrates the technique to be employed when you have a knight against a 'bad' bishop. Note, above all, how in each game the superior side uses his better mobility to infiltrate with his king into the heart of his opponent's position.

A CATALOG OF SELECTED
DOVER BOOKS
IN ALL FIELDS OF INTEREST

A CATALOG OF SELECTED
DOVER BOOKS
IN ALL FIELDS OF INTEREST

DRAWINGS OF REMBRANDT, edited by Seymour Slive. Updated Lippmann, Hofstede de Groot edition, with definitive scholarly apparatus. All portraits, biblical sketches, landscapes, nudes. Oriental figures, classical studies, together with selection of work by followers. 550 illustrations. Total of 630pp. 9⅛ × 12¼.
21485-0, 21486-9 Pa., Two-vol. set $29.90

GHOST AND HORROR STORIES OF AMBROSE BIERCE, Ambrose Bierce. 24 tales vividly imagined, strangely prophetic, and decades ahead of their time in technical skill: "The Damned Thing," "An Inhabitant of Carcosa," "The Eyes of the Panther," "Moxon's Master," and 20 more. 199pp. 5⅜ × 8½. 20767-6 Pa. $4.95

ETHICAL WRITINGS OF MAIMONIDES, Maimonides. Most significant ethical works of great medieval sage, newly translated for utmost precision, readability. Laws Concerning Character Traits, Eight Chapters, more. 192pp. 5⅜ × 8½.
24522-5 Pa. $5.95

THE EXPLORATION OF THE COLORADO RIVER AND ITS CANYONS, J. W. Powell. Full text of Powell's 1,000-mile expedition down the fabled Colorado in 1869. Superb account of terrain, geology, vegetation, Indians, famine, mutiny, treacherous rapids, mighty canyons, during exploration of last unknown part of continental U.S. 400pp. 5⅜ × 8½. 20094-9 Pa. $8.95

HISTORY OF PHILOSOPHY, Julián Marías. Clearest one-volume history on the market. Every major philosopher and dozens of others, to Existentialism and later. 505pp. 5⅜ × 8½. 21739-6 Pa. $9.95

ALL ABOUT LIGHTNING, Martin A. Uman. Highly readable nontechnical survey of nature and causes of lightning, thunderstorms, ball lightning, St. Elmo's Fire, much more. Illustrated. 192pp. 5⅜ × 8½. 25237-X Pa. $5.95

SAILING ALONE AROUND THE WORLD, Captain Joshua Slocum. First man to sail around the world, alone, in small boat. One of great feats of seamanship told in delightful manner. 67 illustrations. 294pp. 5⅜ × 8½. 20326-3 Pa. $4.95

LETTERS AND NOTES ON THE MANNERS, CUSTOMS AND CONDITIONS OF THE NORTH AMERICAN INDIANS, George Catlin. Classic account of life among Plains Indians: ceremonies, hunt, warfare, etc. 312 plates. 572pp. of text. 6⅛ × 9¼. 22118-0, 22119-9, Pa., Two-vol. set $17.90

THE SECRET LIFE OF SALVADOR DALÍ, Salvador Dalí. Outrageous but fascinating autobiography through Dalí's thirties with scores of drawings and sketches and 80 photographs. A must for lovers of 20th-century art. 432pp. 6½ × 9¼. (Available in U.S. only) 27454-3 Pa. $9.95

CATALOG OF DOVER BOOKS

THE BOOK OF BEASTS: Being a Translation from a Latin Bestiary of the Twelfth Century, T. H. White. Wonderful catalog of real and fanciful beasts: manticore, griffin, phoenix, amphivius, jaculus, many more. White's witty erudite commentary on scientific, historical aspects enhances fascinating glimpse of medieval mind. Illustrated. 296pp. 5⅜ × 8¼. (Available in U.S. only)   24609-4 Pa. $7.95

FRANK LLOYD WRIGHT: Architecture and Nature with 160 Illustrations, Donald Hoffmann. Profusely illustrated study of influence of nature—especially prairie—on Wright's designs for Fallingwater, Robie House, Guggenheim Museum, other masterpieces. 96pp. 9¼ × 10¾.   25098-9 Pa. $8.95

LIMBERT ARTS AND CRAFTS FURNITURE: The Complete 1903 Catalog, Charles P. Limbert and Company. Rare catalog depicting 188 pieces of Mission-style furniture: fold-down tables and desks, bookcases, library and octagonal tables, chairs, more. Descriptive captions. 80pp. 9⅜ × 12¼.   27120-X Pa. $6.95

YEARS WITH FRANK LLOYD WRIGHT: Apprentice to Genius, Edgar Tafel. Insightful memoir by a former apprentice presents a revealing portrait of Wright the man, the inspired teacher, the greatest American architect. 372 black-and-white illustrations. Preface. Index. vi + 228pp. 8¼ × 11.   24801-1 Pa. $10.95

THE STORY OF KING ARTHUR AND HIS KNIGHTS, Howard Pyle. Enchanting version of King Arthur fable has delighted generations with imaginative narratives of exciting adventures and unforgettable illustrations by the author. 41 illustrations. xviii + 313pp. 6⅛ × 9¼.   21445-1 Pa. $6.95

THE GODS OF THE EGYPTIANS, E. A. Wallis Budge. Thorough coverage of numerous gods of ancient Egypt by foremost Egyptologist. Information on evolution of cults, rites and gods; the cult of Osiris; the Book of the Dead and its rites; the sacred animals and birds; Heaven and Hell; and more. 956pp. 6⅛ × 9¼.   22055-9, 22056-7 Pa., Two-vol. set $22.90

A THEOLOGICO-POLITICAL TREATISE, Benedict Spinoza. Also contains unfinished *Political Treatise*. Great classic on religious liberty, theory of government on common consent. R. Elwes translation. Total of 421pp. 5⅜ × 8½.   20249-6 Pa. $7.95

INCIDENTS OF TRAVEL IN CENTRAL AMERICA, CHIAPAS, AND YUCATAN, John L. Stephens. Almost single-handed discovery of Maya culture; exploration of ruined cities, monuments, temples; customs of Indians. 115 drawings. 892pp. 5⅜ × 8½.   22404-X, 22405-8 Pa., Two-vol. set $17.90

LOS CAPRICHOS, Francisco Goya. 80 plates of wild, grotesque monsters and caricatures. Prado manuscript included. 183pp. 6⅜ × 9⅜.   22384-1 Pa. $6.95

AUTOBIOGRAPHY: The Story of My Experiments with Truth, Mohandas K. Gandhi. Not hagiography, but Gandhi in his own words. Boyhood, legal studies, purification, the growth of the Satyagraha (nonviolent protest) movement. Critical, inspiring work of the man who freed India. 480pp. 5⅜ × 8½. (Available in U.S. only)   24593-4 Pa. $6.95

ILLUSTRATED DICTIONARY OF HISTORIC ARCHITECTURE, edited by Cyril M. Harris. Extraordinary compendium of clear, concise definitions for over 5,000 important architectural terms complemented by over 2,000 line drawings. Covers full spectrum of architecture from ancient ruins to 20th-century Modernism. Preface. 592pp. 7½ × 9⅜.   24444-X Pa. $15.95

THE NIGHT BEFORE CHRISTMAS, Clement C. Moore. Full text, and woodcuts from original 1848 book. Also critical, historical material. 19 illustrations. 40pp. 4⅝ × 6.   22797-9 Pa. $2.50

THE LESSON OF JAPANESE ARCHITECTURE: 165 Photographs, Jiro Harada. Memorable gallery of 165 photographs taken in the 1930s of exquisite Japanese homes of the well-to-do and historic buildings. 13 line diagrams. 192pp. 8⅜ × 11¼.   24778-3 Pa. $10.95

THE AUTOBIOGRAPHY OF CHARLES DARWIN AND SELECTED LETTERS, edited by Francis Darwin. The fascinating life of eccentric genius composed of an intimate memoir by Darwin (intended for his children); commentary by his son, Francis; hundreds of fragments from notebooks, journals, papers; and letters to and from Lyell, Hooker, Huxley, Wallace and Henslow. xi + 365pp. 5⅜ × 8.
20479-0 Pa. $6.95

WONDERS OF THE SKY: Observing Rainbows, Comets, Eclipses, the Stars and Other Phenomena, Fred Schaaf. Charming, easy-to-read poetic guide to all manner of celestial events visible to the naked eye. Mock suns, glories, Belt of Venus, more. Illustrated. 299pp. 5¼ × 8¼.   24402-4 Pa. $8.95

BURNHAM'S CELESTIAL HANDBOOK, Robert Burnham, Jr. Thorough guide to the stars beyond our solar system. Exhaustive treatment. Alphabetical by constellation: Andromeda to Cetus in Vol. 1; Chamaeleon to Orion in Vol. 2; and Pavo to Vulpecula in Vol. 3. Hundreds of illustrations. Index in Vol. 3. 2,000pp. 6⅛ × 9¼.   23567-X, 23568-8, 23673-0 Pa., Three-vol. set $41.85

STAR NAMES: Their Lore and Meaning, Richard Hinckley Allen. Fascinating history of names various cultures have given to constellations and literary and folkloristic uses that have been made of stars. Indexes to subjects. Arabic and Greek names. Biblical references. Bibliography. 563pp. 5⅜ × 8½.   21079-0 Pa. $9.95

THIRTY YEARS THAT SHOOK PHYSICS: The Story of Quantum Theory, George Gamow. Lucid, accessible introduction to influential theory of energy and matter. Careful explanations of Dirac's anti-particles, Bohr's model of the atom, much more. 12 plates. Numerous drawings. 240pp. 5⅜ × 8½.   24895-X Pa. $6.95

CHINESE DOMESTIC FURNITURE IN PHOTOGRAPHS AND MEASURED DRAWINGS, Gustav Ecke. A rare volume, now affordably priced for antique collectors, furniture buffs and art historians. Detailed review of styles ranging from early Shang to late Ming. Unabridged republication. 161 black-and-white drawings, photos. Total of 224pp. 8⅜ × 11¼. (Available in U.S. only) 25171-3 Pa. $14.95

VINCENT VAN GOGH: A Biography, Julius Meier-Graefe. Dynamic, penetrating study of artist's life, relationship with brother, Theo, painting techniques, travels, more. Readable, engrossing. 160pp. 5⅜ × 8½. (Available in U.S. only)
25253-1 Pa. $4.95

HOW TO WRITE, Gertrude Stein. Gertrude Stein claimed anyone could understand her unconventional writing—here are clues to help. Fascinating improvisations, language experiments, explanations illuminate Stein's craft and the art of writing. Total of 414pp. 4⅝ × 6⅜. 23144-5 Pa. $6.95

ADVENTURES AT SEA IN THE GREAT AGE OF SAIL: Five Firsthand Narratives, edited by Elliot Snow. Rare true accounts of exploration, whaling, shipwreck, fierce natives, trade, shipboard life, more. 33 illustrations. Introduction. 353pp. 5⅜ × 8½. 25177-2 Pa. $9.95

THE HERBAL OR GENERAL HISTORY OF PLANTS, John Gerard. Classic descriptions of about 2,850 plants—with over 2,700 illustrations—includes Latin and English names, physical descriptions, varieties, time and place of growth, more. 2,706 illustrations. xlv + 1,678pp. 8½ × 12¼. 23147-X Cloth. $89.95

DOROTHY AND THE WIZARD IN OZ, L. Frank Baum. Dorothy and the Wizard visit the center of the Earth, where people are vegetables, glass houses grow and Oz characters reappear. Classic sequel to *Wizard of Oz*. 256pp. 5⅜ × 8. 24714-7 Pa. $5.95

SONGS OF EXPERIENCE: Facsimile Reproduction with 26 Plates in Full Color, William Blake. This facsimile of Blake's original "Illuminated Book" reproduces 26 full-color plates from a rare 1826 edition. Includes "The Tyger," "London," "Holy Thursday," and other immortal poems. 26 color plates. Printed text of poems. 48pp. 5¼ × 7. 24636-1 Pa. $3.95

SONGS OF INNOCENCE, William Blake. The first and most popular of Blake's famous "Illuminated Books," in a facsimile edition reproducing all 31 brightly colored plates. Additional printed text of each poem. 64pp. 5¼ × 7. 22764-2 Pa. $3.95

PRECIOUS STONES, Max Bauer. Classic, thorough study of diamonds, rubies, emeralds, garnets, etc.: physical character, occurrence, properties, use, similar topics. 20 plates, 8 in color. 94 figures. 659pp. 6⅛ × 9¼. 21910-0, 21911-9 Pa., Two-vol. set $21.90

ENCYCLOPEDIA OF VICTORIAN NEEDLEWORK, S. F. A. Caulfeild and Blanche Saward. Full, precise descriptions of stitches, techniques for dozens of needlecrafts—most exhaustive reference of its kind. Over 800 figures. Total of 679pp. 8⅛ × 11. 22800-2, 22801-0 Pa., Two-vol. set $26.90

THE MARVELOUS LAND OF OZ, L. Frank Baum. Second Oz book, the Scarecrow and Tin Woodman are back with hero named Tip, Oz magic. 136 illustrations. 287pp. 5⅜ × 8½. 20692-0 Pa. $5.95

WILD FOWL DECOYS, Joel Barber. Basic book on the subject, by foremost authority and collector. Reveals history of decoy making and rigging, place in American culture, different kinds of decoys, how to make them, and how to use them. 140 plates. 156pp. 7⅞ × 10¾. 20011-6 Pa. $14.95

HISTORY OF LACE, Mrs. Bury Palliser. Definitive, profusely illustrated chronicle of lace from earliest times to late 19th century. Laces of Italy, Greece, England, France, Belgium, etc. Landmark of needlework scholarship. 266 illustrations. 672pp. 6⅛ × 9¼. 24742-2 Pa. $16.95

ILLUSTRATED GUIDE TO SHAKER FURNITURE, Robert Meader. All furniture and appurtenances, with much on unknown local styles. 235 photos. 146pp. 9 × 12. 22819-3 Pa. $9.95

WHALE SHIPS AND WHALING: A Pictorial Survey, George Francis Dow. Over 200 vintage engravings, drawings, photographs of barks, brigs, cutters, other vessels. Also harpoons, lances, whaling guns, many other artifacts. Comprehensive text by foremost authority. 207 black-and-white illustrations. 288pp. 6 × 9. 24808-9 Pa. $9.95

THE BERTRAMS, Anthony Trollope. Powerful portrayal of blind self-will and thwarted ambition includes one of Trollope's most heartrending love stories. 497pp. 5⅜ × 8½. 25119-5 Pa. $9.95

ADVENTURES WITH A HAND LENS, Richard Headstrom. Clearly written guide to observing and studying flowers and grasses, fish scales, moth and insect wings, egg cases, buds, feathers, seeds, leaf scars, moss, molds, ferns, common crystals, etc.—all with an ordinary, inexpensive magnifying glass. 209 exact line drawings aid in your discoveries. 220pp. 5⅜ × 8½. 23330-8 Pa. $5.95

RODIN ON ART AND ARTISTS, Auguste Rodin. Great sculptor's candid, wide-ranging comments on meaning of art; great artists; relation of sculpture to poetry, painting, music; philosophy of life, more. 76 superb black-and-white illustrations of Rodin's sculpture, drawings and prints. 119pp. 8⅜ × 11¼. 24487-3 Pa. $7.95

FIFTY CLASSIC FRENCH FILMS, 1912-1982: A Pictorial Record, Anthony Slide. Memorable stills from Grand Illusion, Beauty and the Beast, Hiroshima, Mon Amour, many more. Credits, plot synopses, reviews, etc. 160pp. 8¼ × 11. 25256-6 Pa. $11.95

THE PRINCIPLES OF PSYCHOLOGY, William James. Famous long course complete, unabridged. Stream of thought, time perception, memory, experimental methods; great work decades ahead of its time. 94 figures. 1,391pp. 5⅜ × 8½. 20381-6, 20382-4 Pa., Two-vol. set $25.90

BODIES IN A BOOKSHOP, R. T. Campbell. Challenging mystery of blackmail and murder with ingenious plot and superbly drawn characters. In the best tradition of British suspense fiction. 192pp. 5⅜ × 8½. 24720-1 Pa. $5.95

CALLAS: Portrait of a Prima Donna, George Jellinek. Renowned commentator on the musical scene chronicles incredible career and life of the most controversial, fascinating, influential operatic personality of our time. 64 black-and-white photographs. 416pp. 5⅜ × 8¼. 25047-4 Pa. $8.95

GEOMETRY, RELATIVITY AND THE FOURTH DIMENSION, Rudolph Rucker. Exposition of fourth dimension, concepts of relativity as Flatland characters continue adventures. Popular, easily followed yet accurate, profound. 141 illustrations. 133pp. 5⅜ × 8½. 23400-2 Pa. $4.95

HOUSEHOLD STORIES BY THE BROTHERS GRIMM, with pictures by Walter Crane. 53 classic stories—Rumpelstiltskin, Rapunzel, Hansel and Gretel, the Fisherman and his Wife, Snow White, Tom Thumb, Sleeping Beauty, Cinderella, and so much more—lavishly illustrated with original 19th-century drawings. 114 illustrations. x + 269pp. 5⅜ × 8½. 21080-4 Pa. $4.95

SUNDIALS, Albert Waugh. Far and away the best, most thorough coverage of ideas, mathematics concerned, types, construction, adjusting anywhere. Over 100 illustrations. 230pp. 5⅜ × 8½. 22947-5 Pa. $5.95

PICTURE HISTORY OF THE NORMANDIE: With 190 Illustrations, Frank O. Braynard. Full story of legendary French ocean liner: Art Deco interiors, design innovations, furnishings, celebrities, maiden voyage, tragic fire, much more. Extensive text. 144pp. 8⅞ × 11¾. 25257-4 Pa. $11.95

THE FIRST AMERICAN COOKBOOK: A Facsimile of "American Cookery," 1796, Amelia Simmons. Facsimile of the first American-written cookbook published in the United States contains authentic recipes for colonial favorites—pumpkin pudding, winter squash pudding, spruce beer, Indian slapjacks, and more. Introductory Essay and Glossary of colonial cooking terms. 80pp. 5⅜ × 8½. 24710-4 Pa. $3.50

101 PUZZLES IN THOUGHT AND LOGIC, C. R. Wylie, Jr. Solve murders and robberies, find out which fishermen are liars, how a blind man could possibly identify a color—purely by your own reasoning! 107pp. 5⅜ × 8½. 20367-0 Pa. $2.95

ANCIENT EGYPTIAN MYTHS AND LEGENDS, Lewis Spence. Examines animism, totemism, fetishism, creation myths, deities, alchemy, art and magic, other topics. Over 50 illustrations. 432pp. 5⅜ × 8½. 26525-0 Pa. $8.95

ANTHROPOLOGY AND MODERN LIFE, Franz Boas. Great anthropologist's classic treatise on race and culture. Introduction by Ruth Bunzel. Only inexpensive paperback edition. 255pp. 5⅜ × 8½. 25245-0 Pa. $7.95

THE TALE OF PETER RABBIT, Beatrix Potter. The inimitable Peter's terrifying adventure in Mr. McGregor's garden, with all 27 wonderful, full-color Potter illustrations. 55pp. 4¼ × 5½. 22827-4 Pa. $1.75

THREE PROPHETIC SCIENCE FICTION NOVELS, H. G. Wells. *When the Sleeper Wakes, A Story of the Days to Come* and *The Time Machine* (full version). 335pp. 5⅜ × 8½. (Available in U.S. only) 20605-X Pa. $8.95

APICIUS COOKERY AND DINING IN IMPERIAL ROME, edited and translated by Joseph Dommers Vehling. Oldest known cookbook in existence offers readers a clear picture of what foods Romans ate, how they prepared them, etc. 49 illustrations. 301pp. 6⅛ × 9¼. 23563-7 Pa. $8.95

SHAKESPEARE LEXICON AND QUOTATION DICTIONARY, Alexander Schmidt. Full definitions, locations, shades of meaning of every word in plays and poems. More than 50,000 exact quotations. 1,485pp. 6½ × 9¼. 22726-X, 22727-8 Pa., Two-vol. set $31.90

THE WORLD'S GREAT SPEECHES, edited by Lewis Copeland and Lawrence W. Lamm. Vast collection of 278 speeches from Greeks to 1970. Powerful and effective models; unique look at history. 842pp. 5⅜ × 8½. 20468-5 Pa. $12.95

CATALOG OF DOVER BOOKS

THE BLUE FAIRY BOOK, Andrew Lang. The first, most famous collection, with many familiar tales: Little Red Riding Hood, Aladdin and the Wonderful Lamp, Puss in Boots, Sleeping Beauty, Hansel and Gretel, Rumpelstiltskin; 37 in all. 138 illustrations. 390pp. 5⅜ × 8½.   21437-0 Pa. $6.95

THE STORY OF THE CHAMPIONS OF THE ROUND TABLE, Howard Pyle. Sir Launcelot, Sir Tristram and Sir Percival in spirited adventures of love and triumph retold in Pyle's inimitable style. 50 drawings, 31 full-page. xviii + 329pp. 6½ × 9¼.   21883-X Pa. $7.95

THE MYTHS OF THE NORTH AMERICAN INDIANS, Lewis Spence. Myths and legends of the Algonquins, Iroquois, Pawnees and Sioux with comprehensive historical and ethnological commentary. 36 illustrations. 5⅜ × 8½.
25967-6 Pa. $8.95

GREAT DINOSAUR HUNTERS AND THEIR DISCOVERIES, Edwin H. Colbert. Fascinating, lavishly illustrated chronicle of dinosaur research, 1820s to 1960. Achievements of Cope, Marsh, Brown, Buckland, Mantell, Huxley, many others. 384pp. 5¼ × 8¼.   24701-5 Pa. $8.95

THE TASTEMAKERS, Russell Lynes. Informal, illustrated social history of American taste 1850s–1950s. First popularized categories Highbrow, Lowbrow, Middlebrow. 129 illustrations. New (1979) afterword. 384pp. 6 × 9.
23993-4 Pa. $8.95

NORTH AMERICAN INDIAN LIFE: Customs and Traditions of 23 Tribes, Elsie Clews Parsons (ed.). 27 fictionalized essays by noted anthropologists examine religion, customs, government, additional facets of life among the Winnebago, Crow, Zuni, Eskimo, other tribes. 480pp. 6⅛ × 9¼.   27377-6 Pa. $10.95

AUTHENTIC VICTORIAN DECORATION AND ORNAMENTATION IN FULL COLOR: 46 Plates from "Studies in Design," Christopher Dresser. Superb full-color lithographs reproduced from rare original portfolio of a major Victorian designer. 48pp. 9¼ × 12¼.   25083-0 Pa. $7.95

PRIMITIVE ART, Franz Boas. Remains the best text ever prepared on subject, thoroughly discussing Indian, African, Asian, Australian, and, especially, Northern American primitive art. Over 950 illustrations show ceramics, masks, totem poles, weapons, textiles, paintings, much more. 376pp. 5⅜ × 8.   20025-6 Pa. $8.95

SIDELIGHTS ON RELATIVITY, Albert Einstein. Unabridged republication of two lectures delivered by the great physicist in 1920–21. *Ether and Relativity* and *Geometry and Experience*. Elegant ideas in nonmathematical form, accessible to intelligent layman. vi + 56pp. 5⅜ × 8½.   24511-X Pa. $3.95

THE WIT AND HUMOR OF OSCAR WILDE, edited by Alvin Redman. More than 1,000 ripostes, paradoxes, wisecracks: Work is the curse of the drinking classes, I can resist everything except temptation, etc. 258pp. 5⅜ × 8½.   20602-5 Pa. $4.95

ADVENTURES WITH A MICROSCOPE, Richard Headstrom. 59 adventures with clothing fibers, protozoa, ferns and lichens, roots and leaves, much more. 142 illustrations. 232pp. 5⅜ × 8½.   23471-1 Pa. $4.95

PLANTS OF THE BIBLE, Harold N. Moldenke and Alma L. Moldenke. Standard reference to all 230 plants mentioned in Scriptures. Latin name, biblical reference, uses, modern identity, much more. Unsurpassed encyclopedic resource for scholars, botanists, nature lovers, students of Bible. Bibliography. Indexes. 123 black-and-white illustrations. 384pp. 6 × 9. 25069-5 Pa. $9.95

FAMOUS AMERICAN WOMEN: A Biographical Dictionary from Colonial Times to the Present, Robert McHenry, ed. From Pocahontas to Rosa Parks, 1,035 distinguished American women documented in separate biographical entries. Accurate, up-to-date data, numerous categories, spans 400 years. Indices. 493pp. 6½ × 9¼. 24523-3 Pa. $11.95

THE FABULOUS INTERIORS OF THE GREAT OCEAN LINERS IN HISTORIC PHOTOGRAPHS, William H. Miller, Jr. Some 200 superb photographs capture exquisite interiors of world's great "floating palaces"—1890s to 1980s: *Titanic, Ile de France, Queen Elizabeth, United States, Europa,* more. Approx. 200 black-and-white photographs. Captions. Text. Introduction. 160pp. 8⅞ × 11¾. 24756-2 Pa. $10.95

THE GREAT LUXURY LINERS, 1927–1954: A Photographic Record, William H. Miller, Jr. Nostalgic tribute to heyday of ocean liners. 186 photos of *Ile de France, Normandie, Leviathan, Queen Elizabeth, United States,* many others. Interior and exterior views. Introduction. Captions. 160pp. 9 × 12. 24056-8 Pa. $12.95

A NATURAL HISTORY OF THE DUCKS, John Charles Phillips. Great landmark of ornithology offers complete detailed coverage of nearly 200 species and subspecies of ducks: gadwall, sheldrake, merganser, pintail, many more. 74 full-color plates, 102 black-and-white. Bibliography. Total of 1,920pp. 8⅝ × 11¼. 25141-1, 25142-X Cloth., Two-vol. set $100.00

THE COMPLETE "MASTERS OF THE POSTER": All 256 Color Plates from "Les Maîtres de l'Affiche", Stanley Appelbaum (ed.). The most famous compilation ever made of the art of the great age of the poster, featuring works by Chéret, Steinlen, Toulouse-Lautrec, nearly 100 other artists. One poster per page. 272pp. 9¼ × 12¼. 26309-6 Pa. $29.95

THE TEN BOOKS OF ARCHITECTURE: The 1755 Leoni Edition, Leon Battista Alberti. Rare classic helped introduce the glories of ancient architecture to the Renaissance. 68 black-and-white plates. 336pp. 8⅜ × 11¼. 25239-6 Pa. $14.95

MISS MACKENZIE, Anthony Trollope. Minor masterpieces by Victorian master unmasks many truths about life in 19th-century England. First inexpensive edition in years. 392pp. 5⅜ × 8½. 25201-9 Pa. $8.95

THE RIME OF THE ANCIENT MARINER, Gustave Doré, Samuel Taylor Coleridge. Dramatic engravings considered by many to be his greatest work. The terrifying space of the open sea, the storms and whirlpools of an unknown ocean, the ice of Antarctica, more—all rendered in a powerful, chilling manner. Full text. 38 plates. 77pp. 9¼ × 12. 22305-1 Pa. $4.95

THE EXPEDITIONS OF ZEBULON MONTGOMERY PIKE, Zebulon Montgomery Pike. Fascinating firsthand accounts (1805–6) of exploration of Mississippi River, Indian wars, capture by Spanish dragoons, much more. 1,088pp. 5⅜ × 8½. 25254-X, 25255-8 Pa., Two-vol. set $25.90

A CONCISE HISTORY OF PHOTOGRAPHY: Third Revised Edition, Helmut Gernsheim. Best one-volume history—camera obscura, photochemistry, daguerreotypes, evolution of cameras, film, more. Also artistic aspects—landscape, portraits, fine art, etc. 281 black-and-white photographs. 26 in color. 176pp. 8⅜ × 11¼.
25128-4 Pa. $14.95

THE DORÉ BIBLE ILLUSTRATIONS, Gustave Doré. 241 detailed plates from the Bible: the Creation scenes, Adam and Eve, Flood, Babylon, battle sequences, life of Jesus, etc. Each plate is accompanied by the verses from the King James version of the Bible. 241pp. 9 × 12.
23004-X Pa. $9.95

WANDERINGS IN WEST AFRICA, Richard F. Burton. Great Victorian scholar/adventurer's invaluable descriptions of African tribal rituals, fetishism, culture, art, much more. Fascinating 19th-century account. 624pp. 5⅜ × 8½. 26890-X Pa. $12.95

HISTORIC HOMES OF THE AMERICAN PRESIDENTS, Second Revised Edition, Irvin Haas. Guide to homes occupied by every president from Washington to Bush. Visiting hours, travel routes, more. 175 photos. 160pp. 8¼ × 11.
26751-2 Pa. $9.95

THE HISTORY OF THE LEWIS AND CLARK EXPEDITION, Meriwether Lewis and William Clark, edited by Elliott Coues. Classic edition of Lewis and Clark's day-by-day journals that later became the basis for U.S. claims to Oregon and the West. Accurate and invaluable geographical, botanical, biological, meteorological and anthropological material. Total of 1,508pp. 5⅜ × 8½.
21268-8, 21269-6, 21270-X Pa., Three-vol. set $29.85

LANGUAGE, TRUTH AND LOGIC, Alfred J. Ayer. Famous, clear introduction to Vienna, Cambridge schools of Logical Positivism. Role of philosophy, elimination of metaphysics, nature of analysis, etc. 160pp. 5⅜ × 8½. (Available in U.S. and Canada only)
20010-8 Pa. $3.95

MATHEMATICS FOR THE NONMATHEMATICIAN, Morris Kline. Detailed, college-level treatment of mathematics in cultural and historical context, with numerous exercises. For liberal arts students. Preface. Recommended Reading Lists. Tables. Index. Numerous black-and-white figures. xvi + 641pp. 5⅜ × 8½.
24823-2 Pa. $11.95

HANDBOOK OF PICTORIAL SYMBOLS, Rudolph Modley. 3,250 signs and symbols, many systems in full; official or heavy commercial use. Arranged by subject. Most in Pictorial Archive series. 143pp. 8¼ × 11. 23357-X Pa. $8.95

INCIDENTS OF TRAVEL IN YUCATAN, John L. Stephens. Classic (1843) exploration of jungles of Yucatan, looking for evidences of Maya civilization. Travel adventures, Mexican and Indian culture, etc. Total of 669pp. 5⅜ × 8½.
20926-1, 20927-X Pa., Two-vol. set $13.90

CATALOG OF DOVER BOOKS

DEGAS: An Intimate Portrait, Ambroise Vollard. Charming, anecdotal memoir by famous art dealer of one of the greatest 19th-century French painters. 14 black-and-white illustrations. Introduction by Harold L. Van Doren. 96pp. 5⅜ × 8½.
25131-4 Pa. $4.95

PERSONAL NARRATIVE OF A PILGRIMAGE TO AL-MADINAH AND MECCAH, Richard F. Burton. Great travel classic by remarkably colorful personality. Burton, disguised as a Moroccan, visited sacred shrines of Islam, narrowly escaping death. 47 illustrations. 959pp. 5⅜ × 8½.
21217-3, 21218-1 Pa., Two-vol. set $19.90

PHRASE AND WORD ORIGINS, A. H. Holt. Entertaining, reliable, modern study of more than 1,200 colorful words, phrases, origins and histories. Much unexpected information. 254pp. 5⅜ × 8½.
20758-7 Pa. $5.95

THE RED THUMB MARK, R. Austin Freeman. In this first Dr. Thorndyke case, the great scientific detective draws fascinating conclusions from the nature of a single fingerprint. Exciting story, authentic science. 320pp. 5⅜ × 8½. (Available in U.S. only)
25210-8 Pa. $6.95

AN EGYPTIAN HIEROGLYPHIC DICTIONARY, E. A. Wallis Budge. Monumental work containing about 25,000 words or terms that occur in texts ranging from 3000 B.C. to 600 A.D. Each entry consists of a transliteration of the word, the word in hieroglyphs, and the meaning in English. 1,314pp. 6⅞ × 10.
23615-3, 23616-1 Pa., Two-vol. set $35.90

THE COMPLEAT STRATEGYST: Being a Primer on the Theory of Games of Strategy, J. D. Williams. Highly entertaining classic describes, with many illustrated examples, how to select best strategies in conflict situations. Prefaces. Appendices. xvi + 268pp. 5⅜ × 8½.
25101-2 Pa. $7.95

THE ROAD TO OZ, L. Frank Baum. Dorothy meets the Shaggy Man, little Button-Bright and the Rainbow's beautiful daughter in this delightful trip to the magical Land of Oz. 272pp. 5⅜ × 8.
25208-6 Pa. $5.95

POINT AND LINE TO PLANE, Wassily Kandinsky. Seminal exposition of role of point, line, other elements in nonobjective painting. Essential to understanding 20th-century art. 127 illustrations. 192pp. 6½ × 9¼.
23808-3 Pa. $5.95

LADY ANNA, Anthony Trollope. Moving chronicle of Countess Lovel's bitter struggle to win for herself and daughter Anna their rightful rank and fortune—perhaps at cost of sanity itself. 384pp. 5⅜ × 8½.
24669-8 Pa. $8.95

EGYPTIAN MAGIC, E. A. Wallis Budge. Sums up all that is known about magic in Ancient Egypt: the role of magic in controlling the gods, powerful amulets that warded off evil spirits, scarabs of immortality, use of wax images, formulas and spells, the secret name, much more. 253pp. 5⅜ × 8½.
22681-6 Pa. $4.95

THE DANCE OF SIVA, Ananda Coomaraswamy. Preeminent authority unfolds the vast metaphysic of India: the revelation of her art, conception of the universe, social organization, etc. 27 reproductions of art masterpieces. 192pp. 5⅜ × 8½.
24817-8 Pa. $6.95

CHRISTMAS CUSTOMS AND TRADITIONS, Clement A. Miles. Origin, evolution, significance of religious, secular practices. Caroling, gifts, yule logs, much more. Full, scholarly yet fascinating; non-sectarian. 400pp. 5⅜ × 8½.
23354-5 Pa. $7.95

THE HUMAN FIGURE IN MOTION, Eadweard Muybridge. More than 4,500 stopped-action photos, in action series, showing undraped men, women, children jumping, lying down, throwing, sitting, wrestling, carrying, etc. 390pp. 7⅞ × 10⅝.
20204-6 Cloth. $24.95

THE MAN WHO WAS THURSDAY, Gilbert Keith Chesterton. Witty, fast-paced novel about a club of anarchists in turn-of-the-century London. Brilliant social, religious, philosophical speculations. 128pp. 5⅜ × 8½. 25121-7 Pa. $3.95

A CÉZANNE SKETCHBOOK: Figures, Portraits, Landscapes and Still Lifes, Paul Cézanne. Great artist experiments with tonal effects, light, mass, other qualities in over 100 drawings. A revealing view of developing master painter, precursor of Cubism. 102 black-and-white illustrations. 144pp. 8¾ × 6⅜. 24790-2 Pa. $6.95

AN ENCYCLOPEDIA OF BATTLES: Accounts of Over 1,560 Battles from 1479 B.C. to the Present, David Eggenberger. Presents essential details of every major battle in recorded history, from the first battle of Megiddo in 1479 B.C. to Grenada in 1984. List of Battle Maps. New Appendix covering the years 1967–1984. Index. 99 illustrations. 544pp. 6½ × 9¼. 24913-1 Pa. $14.95

AN ETYMOLOGICAL DICTIONARY OF MODERN ENGLISH, Ernest Weekley. Richest, fullest work, by foremost British lexicographer. Detailed word histories. Inexhaustible. Total of 856pp. 6½ × 9¼.
21873-2, 21874-0 Pa., Two-vol. set $19.90

WEBSTER'S AMERICAN MILITARY BIOGRAPHIES, edited by Robert McHenry. Over 1,000 figures who shaped 3 centuries of American military history. Detailed biographies of Nathan Hale, Douglas MacArthur, Mary Hallaren, others. Chronologies of engagements, more. Introduction. Addenda. 1,033 entries in alphabetical order. xi + 548pp. 6½ × 9¼. (Available in U.S. only)
24758-9 Pa. $13.95

LIFE IN ANCIENT EGYPT, Adolf Erman. Detailed older account, with much not in more recent books: domestic life, religion, magic, medicine, commerce, and whatever else needed for complete picture. Many illustrations. 597pp. 5⅜ × 8½.
22632-8 Pa. $9.95

HISTORIC COSTUME IN PICTURES, Braun & Schneider. Over 1,450 costumed figures shown, covering a wide variety of peoples: kings, emperors, nobles, priests, servants, soldiers, scholars, townsfolk, peasants, merchants, courtiers, cavaliers, and more. 256pp. 8⅜ × 11¼. 23150-X Pa. $9.95

THE NOTEBOOKS OF LEONARDO DA VINCI, edited by J. P. Richter. Extracts from manuscripts reveal great genius; on painting, sculpture, anatomy, sciences, geography, etc. Both Italian and English. 186 ms. pages reproduced, plus 500 additional drawings, including studies for *Last Supper, Sforza* monument, etc. 860pp. 7⅞ × 10¾. 22572-0, 22573-9 Pa., Two-vol. set $35.90

CATALOG OF DOVER BOOKS

THE ART NOUVEAU STYLE BOOK OF ALPHONSE MUCHA: All 72 Plates from "Documents Decoratifs" in Original Color, Alphonse Mucha. Rare copyright-free design portfolio by high priest of Art Nouveau. Jewelry, wallpaper, stained glass, furniture, figure studies, plant and animal motifs, etc. Only complete one-volume edition. 80pp. 9⅜ × 12¼. 24044-4 Pa. $10.95

ANIMALS: 1,419 Copyright-Free Illustrations of Mammals, Birds, Fish, Insects, Etc., edited by Jim Harter. Clear wood engravings present, in extremely lifelike poses, over 1,000 species of animals. One of the most extensive pictorial sourcebooks of its kind. Captions. Index. 284pp. 9 × 12. 23766-4 Pa. $10.95

OBELISTS FLY HIGH, C. Daly King. Masterpiece of American detective fiction, long out of print, involves murder on a 1935 transcontinental flight—"a very thrilling story"—NY Times. Unabridged and unaltered republication of the edition published by William Collins Sons & Co. Ltd., London, 1935. 288pp. 5⅜ × 8½. (Available in U.S. only) 25036-9 Pa. $5.95

VICTORIAN AND EDWARDIAN FASHION: A Photographic Survey, Alison Gernsheim. First fashion history completely illustrated by contemporary photographs. Full text plus 235 photos, 1840-1914, in which many celebrities appear. 240pp. 6½ × 9¼. 24205-6 Pa. $8.95

THE ART OF THE FRENCH ILLUSTRATED BOOK, 1700-1914, Gordon N. Ray. Over 630 superb book illustrations by Fragonard, Delacroix, Daumier, Doré, Grandville, Manet, Mucha, Steinlen, Toulouse-Lautrec and many others. Preface. Introduction. 633 halftones. Indices of artists, authors & titles, binders and provenances. Appendices. Bibliography. 608pp. 8⅜ × 11¼. 25086-5 Pa. $24.95

THE WONDERFUL WIZARD OF OZ, L. Frank Baum. Facsimile in full color of America's finest children's classic. 143 illustrations by W. W. Denslow. 267pp. 5⅜ × 8½. 20691-2 Pa. $7.95

FOLLOWING THE EQUATOR: A Journey Around the World, Mark Twain. Great writer's 1897 account of circumnavigating the globe by steamship. Ironic humor, keen observations, vivid and fascinating descriptions of exotic places. 197 illustrations. 720pp. 5⅜ × 8½. 26113-1 Pa. $15.95

THE FRIENDLY STARS, Martha Evans Martin & Donald Howard Menzel. Classic text marshalls the stars together in an engaging, nontechnical survey, presenting them as sources of beauty in night sky. 23 illustrations. Foreword. 2 star charts. Index. 147pp. 5⅜ × 8½. 21099-5 Pa. $3.95

FADS AND FALLACIES IN THE NAME OF SCIENCE, Martin Gardner. Fair, witty appraisal of cranks, quacks, and quackeries of science and pseudoscience: hollow earth, Velikovsky, orgone energy, Dianetics, flying saucers, Bridey Murphy, food and medical fads, etc. Revised, expanded In the Name of Science. "A very able and even-tempered presentation."—The New Yorker. 363pp. 5⅜ × 8. 20394-8 Pa. $6.95

ANCIENT EGYPT: Its Culture and History, J. E. Manchip White. From predynastics through Ptolemies: society, history, political structure, religion, daily life, literature, cultural heritage. 48 plates. 217pp. 5⅜ × 8½. 22548-8 Pa. $5.95

CATALOG OF DOVER BOOKS

SIR HARRY HOTSPUR OF HUMBLETHWAITE, Anthony Trollope. Incisive, unconventional psychological study of a conflict between a wealthy baronet, his idealistic daughter, and their scapegrace cousin. The 1870 novel in its first inexpensive edition in years. 250pp. 5⅜ × 8½.   24953-0 Pa. $6.95

LASERS AND HOLOGRAPHY, Winston E. Kock. Sound introduction to burgeoning field, expanded (1981) for second edition. Wave patterns, coherence, lasers, diffraction, zone plates, properties of holograms, recent advances. 84 illustrations. 160pp. 5⅜ × 8¼. (Except in United Kingdom)   24041-X Pa. $4.95

INTRODUCTION TO ARTIFICIAL INTELLIGENCE: Second, Enlarged Edition, Philip C. Jackson, Jr. Comprehensive survey of artificial intelligence—the study of how machines (computers) can be made to act intelligently. Includes introductory and advanced material. Extensive notes updating the main text. 132 black-and-white illustrations. 512pp. 5⅜ × 8½.   24864-X Pa. $10.95

HISTORY OF INDIAN AND INDONESIAN ART, Ananda K. Coomaraswamy. Over 400 illustrations illuminate classic study of Indian art from earliest Harappa finds to early 20th century. Provides philosophical, religious and social insights. 304pp. 6⅜ × 9⅜.   25005-9 Pa. $11.95

THE GOLEM, Gustav Meyrink. Most famous supernatural novel in modern European literature, set in Ghetto of Old Prague around 1890. Compelling story of mystical experiences, strange transformations, profound terror. 13 black-and-white illustrations. 224pp. 5⅜ × 8½.   25025-3 Pa. $7.95

PICTORIAL ENCYCLOPEDIA OF HISTORIC ARCHITECTURAL PLANS, DETAILS AND ELEMENTS: With 1,880 Line Drawings of Arches, Domes, Doorways, Facades, Gables, Windows, etc., John Theodore Haneman. Sourcebook of inspiration for architects, designers, others. Bibliography. Captions. 141pp. 9×12.
                                                             24605-1 Pa. $8.95

BENCHLEY LOST AND FOUND, Robert Benchley. Finest humor from early 30s, about pet peeves, child psychologists, post office and others. Mostly unavailable elsewhere. 73 illustrations by Peter Arno and others. 183pp. 5⅜ × 8½.
                                                             22410-4 Pa. $4.95

ERTÉ GRAPHICS, Erté. Collection of striking color graphics: *Seasons, Alphabet, Numerals, Aces* and *Precious Stones*. 50 plates, including 4 on covers. 48pp. 9⅜×12¼.
                                                             23580-7 Pa. $7.95

THE JOURNAL OF HENRY D. THOREAU, edited by Bradford Torrey, F. H. Allen. Complete reprinting of 14 volumes, 1837–61, over two million words; the sourcebooks for *Walden*, etc. Definitive. All original sketches, plus 75 photographs. 1,804pp. 8½ × 12¼.   20312-3, 20313-1 Cloth., Two-vol. set $130.00

CASTLES: Their Construction and History, Sidney Toy. Traces castle development from ancient roots. Nearly 200 photographs and drawings illustrate moats, keeps, baileys, many other features. Caernarvon, Dover Castles, Hadrian's Wall, Tower of London, dozens more. 256pp. 5⅜ × 8¼.   24898-4 Pa. $7.95

AMERICAN CLIPPER SHIPS: 1833–1858, Octavius T. Howe & Frederick C. Matthews. Fully-illustrated, encyclopedic review of 352 clipper ships from the period of America's greatest maritime supremacy. Introduction. 109 halftones. 5 black-and-white line illustrations. Index. Total of 928pp. 5⅜ × 8½.
25115-2, 25116-0 Pa., Two-vol. set $21.90

TOWARDS A NEW ARCHITECTURE, Le Corbusier. Pioneering manifesto by great architect, near legendary founder of "International School." Technical and aesthetic theories, views on industry, economics, relation of form to function, "mass-production spirit," much more. Profusely illustrated. Unabridged translation of 13th French edition. Introduction by Frederick Etchells. 320pp. 6⅛ × 9¼.
(Available in U.S. only) 25023-7 Pa. $8.95

THE BOOK OF KELLS, edited by Blanche Cirker. Inexpensive collection of 32 full-color, full-page plates from the greatest illuminated manuscript of the Middle Ages, painstakingly reproduced from rare facsimile edition. Publisher's Note. Captions. 32pp. 9⅜ × 12¼. (Available in U.S. only) 24345-1 Pa. $5.95

BEST SCIENCE FICTION STORIES OF H. G. WELLS, H. G. Wells. Full novel *The Invisible Man*, plus 17 short stories: "The Crystal Egg," "Aepyornis Island," "The Strange Orchid," etc. 303pp. 5⅜ × 8½. (Available in U.S. only)
21531-8 Pa. $6.95

AMERICAN SAILING SHIPS: Their Plans and History, Charles G. Davis. Photos, construction details of schooners, frigates, clippers, other sailcraft of 18th to early 20th centuries—plus entertaining discourse on design, rigging, nautical lore, much more. 137 black-and-white illustrations. 240pp. 6⅛ × 9¼.
24658-2 Pa. $6.95

ENTERTAINING MATHEMATICAL PUZZLES, Martin Gardner. Selection of author's favorite conundrums involving arithmetic, money, speed, etc., with lively commentary. Complete solutions. 112pp. 5⅜ × 8½. 25211-6 Pa. $3.95

THE WILL TO BELIEVE, HUMAN IMMORTALITY, William James. Two books bound together. Effect of irrational on logical, and arguments for human immortality. 402pp. 5⅜ × 8½. 20291-7 Pa. $8.95

THE HAUNTED MONASTERY and THE CHINESE MAZE MURDERS, Robert Van Gulik. 2 full novels by Van Gulik continue adventures of Judge Dee and his companions. An evil Taoist monastery, seemingly supernatural events; overgrown topiary maze that hides strange crimes. Set in 7th-century China. 27 illustrations. 328pp. 5⅜ × 8½. 23502-5 Pa. $6.95

CELEBRATED CASES OF JUDGE DEE (DEE GOONG AN), translated by Robert Van Gulik. Authentic 18th-century Chinese detective novel; Dee and associates solve three interlocked cases. Led to Van Gulik's own stories with same characters. Extensive introduction. 9 illustrations. 237pp. 5⅜ × 8½.
23337-5 Pa. $5.95

Prices subject to change without notice.

Available at your book dealer or write for free catalog to Dept. GI, Dover Publications, Inc., 31 East 2nd St., Mineola, N.Y. 11501. Dover publishes more than 400 books each year on science, elementary and advanced mathematics, biology, music, art, literary history, social sciences and other areas.